Come for Cocktails, Stay for Supper

Come for Cocktails, Stay for Supper

MARIAN BURROS
LOIS LEVINE

ILLUSTRATIONS BY *Rosalie Petrash Schmidt*

THE MACMILLAN COMPANY
COLLIER-MACMILLAN LTD., LONDON

The Macmillan Company
866 Third Avenue, New York, N.Y. 10022
Collier-Macmillan Canada Ltd., Toronto, Ontario

Printed in the United States of America

To S.L.L. and D.D.G.

Contents

Introduction

Come for cocktails, stay for supper. We're feeding you more than peanuts and popcorn, cold, salty ham and rubbery turkey.

Over the years, so-called cocktail parties have become so elaborate, and extended so far into the evening, that a new form of entertaining has sprung up requiring the invention of a new, hyphenated word—cocktail-buffet.

It's a catchall phrase used to describe a party at which you can expect enough to eat so that you don't have to go elsewhere to fill in the holes left by just potato chips and a dip. Whether it was the cocktail party or the buffet dinner that turned into the cocktail-buffet depends on whom you ask. Those who wanted to do more than give you just a drink added some cold meats, perhaps a hot dish, a salad and a dessert. Those who believed only in formal, sit-down dinners, but could no longer find the right kind of help, extended the cocktail hour, served help-yourself foods and discovered they liked the informality of it all.

The cocktail-buffet is loaded with pluses. The quantity of people who can be entertained is considerably larger than at a seated dinner, and the amount and quality of the hired help can be trimmed. Each guest is free to move around and mingle instead of possibly being stuck with an incompatible and boring dinner partner. Since there are always those who would rather continue the cocktail hour than go to the buffet, all the service is not required at one time. The cocktail-buffet is very much in keeping with today's breezy, informal style of living.

However, many hostesses cling to a custom that is very confusing. An invitation to a cocktail-buffet is an invitation to stay the evening, yet many women are guilty of sending out invitations that read: *Cocktail-buffet. From 6 to 8!* People have learned to interpret this pretty well by now, but for a long time there were embarrassed guests who had made other plans for the evening and were caught sneaking out the door. An invitation for cocktails only should let you know when to leave, while an invitation to a cocktail-buffet, just as to a dinner, should read: *From* or *At* (whatever hour you choose).

But for mass entertaining nothing beats the traditional cocktail party. So it is still very much in evidence. It serves other functions as well: for entertaining before a dinner dance, before going on to a restaurant for dinner, or when there will be a midnight supper after an event. In any of these instances, cocktails at home are just the ticket. Before a dinner the hors d'oeuvres should be simple and light. But if no food is to be served until midnight, they should be more substantial. Growling stomachs in a theater audience are distracting.

At a cocktail party the menu consists only of hors d'oeuvres. For a small crowd, say ten people, a selection of two hot and one cold hors d'oeuvre is ample. For a group of twenty to forty, six to eight different kinds are needed. At a large cocktail party of forty or more, at least eight recipes for hors d'oeuvres should be provided in order to have a varied selection.

And what's a cocktail hour without a drink! So in addition to providing you with party menus and recipes, as well as information on how to serve easily and attractively, we've included suggestions for organizing your bar with some guide lines on how much liquor is needed and what constitutes a well-stocked bar. For good measure we've included a few really great recipes for mixed drinks and punches.

It doesn't take more than one or two parties in a new city to discover what the drinking preferences are, and they vary from section to section. Generally speaking, most people prefer straight whiskey, and in the Northeast and Middle-Atlantic states, scotch is first choice, followed by bourbon. Bourbon comes up first as you move south. So scotch and bourbon with soda and ginger ale as mixers are the basic ingredients of the simplest bar.

Those who drink cocktails seem to stand mostly for the martini, whether gin or vodka. In addition to the gin and vodka, then, there has to be a bottle of dry vermouth. And don't forget the onions, olives, and lemon peel twists.

The well-stocked bar should include blended whiskey, often known as rye, and sherry, plus tomato and orange juices. Carbonated mixtures of lemon, lime, and grapefruit, and quinine water in warm weather, also may be used for tall drinks. And don't forget the ingredients for the Bloody Marys! The thoughtful hostess will also stock soft drinks for the "nons."

In the cocktail department the variety is endless, but we have included recipes for our favorites: the martini, daiquiri, Marguerita, whiskey sour, Bloody Mary, and champagne punch. And for those of you who will have to add to your bar, supplies are indicated in the particular recipes.

Unless you have a professional bartender on hand, you will not want to offer a choice of too many mixed drinks at one party. Stick to the highballs and perhaps one cocktail that can be premixed successfully. If you do plan on professional help, figure on one man to each thirty to fifty guests and still do not allow unlimited choice of drinks.

On the glassware shelf you will need highball glasses, old-fashioned glasses, and stemmed cocktail glasses. Or you can make double old-fashioned glasses do double duty for long and on-the-rocks drinks. You may wish to add sherry and cordial glasses too.

Basic bar equipment should include a corkscrew, a can opener as well as a bottle opener, jigger, pitcher, cocktail shaker, wire strainer, measuring spoons, stirrers, and paring knife. Some of this equipment can be lifted from the kitchen as needed.

Most important is ice and a generous-sized ice bucket. Have more ice cubes than you can possibly use stored in your freezer or in insulated bags. Ice is an inexpensive and simple ingredient to stock up on and an unforgivable sin as well as darned nuisance to run out of in the middle of a party. Figure on a pound of ice per person.

How many drinks do you plan on? Well, it depends on your crowd, on the weather, and the mood of the evening, which you can never guess in advance. But generally we use the following chart as a guide. Remember, though, liquor has a long shelf life.

Better to have too much. And don't forget that most liquor stores will allow you to return unopened bottles if you have requested permission in advance.

if you're having	predinner cocktails average		party average	
	drinks	quarts	drinks	quarts
4 people	10–14	1	14–18	2
6 people	14–20	2	20–26	2
8 people	18–26	2	26–34	3
12 people	26–38	3	38–50	4
20 people	42–62	4	62–82	6
25 people	50–74	5	74–98	7
40 people	82–122	8	122–162	11

The next question is how much liquor do you get from a bottle (quart)? Measurements are in quarts since they are more economical than fifths and take up little extra space. Also quarts are easier to handle than half-gallons. For that we have provided still another handy reference.

Whiskey
  19 highballs   16 manhattans   20 sours or old fashioneds
Sweet vermouth
  32 manhattans   25 on the rocks
Dry vermouth
  75 martinis   25 on the rocks
Gin
  16 martinis   20 gin and tonics
Vodka
  16 martinis   20 Bloody Marys
Cordials or liqueurs
  31 after-dinner drinks
Cognac or brandy
  20 highballs   38 ponies
Champagne (26 ounces)
  8 glasses

Staying at the bar for a moment or two before moving into the kitchen, we offer the recipes for the drinks most people request:

Martini

   2½ ounces gin
   ½ ounce dry vermouth
   2–3 ice cubes
   lemon twist or olive

Stir ingredients together in a glass pitcher, using glass rod. Strain into cocktail glass, dressed with twist of lemon or olive. If dressing is pearl onion, the drink is called a *gibson*.

Whiskey Sour

   2 dashes bitters
   1½ ounces blended whiskey
   ¾ ounce lemon juice
   1 slice orange
   maraschino cherry
   crushed ice
   1 teaspoon fine granulated sugar

Shake well with ice and strain into glass prepared with a slice of orange and cherry.

Daiquiri

Juice of ½ lime
2 ounces light rum
crushed ice
1 scant teaspoon sugar*

Shake well with ice, strain into cocktail glass. For frozen daiquiri shake with ice and serve unstrained with short straws in "saucer" champagne glass.

* A simple sugar syrup may be made by boiling for 5 minutes:
4 cups sugar
1 cup water

A half ounce syrup equals 1 scant teaspoon sugar and will taste smoother in your drink.

Bloody Mary

1½ ounces vodka
1 dash Worcestershire sauce
1 drop hot pepper sauce
3 ounces tomato juice
½ ounce lemon juice
salt and pepper to taste
crushed ice

Shake well with ice. Strain into highball glass.

Marguerita

1½ ounces white tequila
½ ounce triple sec
1 ounce lemon juice
salt
crushed ice

Shake with ice and serve in salt-rimmed glass prepared by rubbing rim with cut lemon and dipping in salt.

Champagne Punch

For 50 4-ounce servings
3 (⅘-quart) bottles dry white dinner wine
2 (46-ounce) cans pineapple-grapefruit juice
2 (6-ounce) cans frozen lemonade concentrate
2 (26-ounce) bottles champagne

Chill all ingredients well. Combine wine and fruit juices in punch bowl with a small block of ice. Pour champagne in just before serving.

A few well-chosen toasts and we're all set . . .

Not only what you serve but how you serve it is important. Hot hors d'oeuvres should be piping hot, cold ones fresh and well chilled, never soggy.

Hot foods stay hot in chafing dishes or on electric hot trays which keep food warm without further cooking. Candle warmers under fireproof dishes will do the trick in the simplest and least expensive way.

To keep raw vegetables cold and crisp, serve them in the center of an ice ring. And never put out too much food at a time. It will lose its freshness by prolonged exposure.

When you buy serving pieces, try to be practical. Those that go from oven to table make the most sense, whether they are elegant,

glass-lined silver serving pieces or vividly painted earthenware casseroles. Today a well-appointed table has nothing to do with cost.

If you are lucky enough to have help passing and serving the
food, you will need one person in the living room, for about fifty
guests, and at least one in the kitchen helping to heat the food
and refresh the trays. With a crowd of fifty or more, hired help
is almost mandatory. Of course, if you have children of the right
age who love to "make the scene," they should be pressed into
service if they promise to be neat and quiet and not eat too much.
A friend recently commented that she always puts her children to
work, since guests aren't half so critical when children pass the
food!

The recipes in this book have been designed so that most of
the cooking can be done long before the party. We have once
again used our favorite method of marking recipes to let you know
about advance preparation. (For who wants to be stuck in the
kitchen when the company is arriving?) An asterisk * means a
recipe is freezable—it can be prepared at least two weeks ahead.
The number sign # with a 1, 2, or 3 beside it indicates how many
days ahead a recipe may be safely prepared and refrigerated without losing any of its quality or appeal.

Each recipe is individually marked to let you know how many
it will serve so that you can follow our suggested menus or switch
a menu if you want to. For example, at a party for twelve, you
would need eight helpings of a sea food casserole and eight helpings of a meat dish rather than twelve portions of each, which
would be too much. If you want to eliminate the sea food, you
would increase the meat; if you want to substitute poultry for
sea food, you will have to find a recipe also serving eight. But substitute carefully. Sauces on every dish, nothing but casseroles, or
too many dishes with wine are not aesthetically pleasing to look
at or digest.

We have suggested menus using many, but not nearly all, of
these new recipes. The menus not only tell how many they will
serve, but also their general style: informal or formal, seated or
stand up, light or heavy, even a suggested time of year. No menu,
of course, is ironbound, and you may certainly change a menu as
you wish.

As always, the recipes are home-, husband-, and guest-tested. And as always they are elegant to serve because they are easy to prepare. So don't hesitate to invite your friends to come for cocktails and stay for supper.

Menus

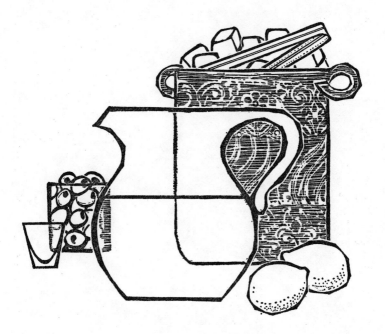

Cocktail-Buffet Menus

Hearty   Winter   Knives and Forks   Serves 8
Chicken Sticks
Molded Guacamole
Peppy Almonds
Neapolitan Veal
Lisa's Noodles
Celery Heart Salad
Ginger Coffee Treat

Informal   Winter   Forks only   Serves 8
Hot Frijole Chip Dip
Zippy Avocado
Sour-Cream Noodle Bake
Fisherman's Find
Barbecued French Loaf
Wellesley Coffee Cake

Casual and Hearty   Winter   Forks only   Serves 8
South-of-the-Border Dip
Chutney Olive Dip
Beef 'n' Beer
Chesapeake Crab
Ensalada de Arroz
Cheddar Corn Bread
Toffee Ice Cream Roll

Stand Up   Winter   Forks only   Serves 12
Chesapeake Clams and Cheese
Sunshine Sausage Rolls
Toasted Almond Dip
Veal Flamenco
Swedish Chicken Salad
Wilted Cucumber Slices
Herb Ring-a-Round
Fyrste Kake
Sweet Potato Pecan Cake

Oriental   Winter   Knives and Forks   Serves 12
Ham and Pineapple Savories
Pickled Mushrooms
Sassy Pecans
Beef with Oyster Sauce
Chicken Lo Mein
Exotic Shrimp Salad
Celery with Waterchestnuts
Baked Fruit Dessert
Almond Tea Cakes

Sunday Night   Winter   Informal   Knives and Forks   Serves 8
Onion Cheese Wafers
Down East Sardine Mold
Cassoulet
Lemon Pepper Tomatoes
Tangy Cucumber Ring
Smoky Bread
Paragon Queen's Heart

Elegant   Spring   Forks only   Serves 8
Vienna Pinwheels
Shrimp Pâté
Cannelloni
Artichoke Bottoms Filled with Peas
Pineapple Daiquiri Mold
Coffee Almond Cream Pie

Stand Up Spring Forks only Serves 12
Oriental Shrimp
Wurst-stuffed Mushrooms
Basic Black and Gold
South Sea Beef
Chicken Livers Gourmet
Betsy's Spinach
Tomato Ring
Marble Brownies
Miniature Cheesecakes
Danish Sugar Cookies

Sit-Down Spring Knives and Forks Serves 12
Mushrooms Stuffed with Anchovies
Black Olive Dip
Pier 4 Cheese Spread
Veal Marengo
Paella Salad
Zucchini au Gratin
Filbert Torte
Almond Tart

Fairly Elegant Spring Knives and Forks Serves 12
Spinach Cheese Rolls
Ceci Rémoulade
Cheese 'n' Chutney
Tomato Glazed Beef
Scallop Casserole
Artichoke Hearts and Peas
Sparkling Salad Mold
Frozen Macaroon Soufflé

Informal Spring Forks only Serves 8
Chef's Favorite
Green Goddess Dip
Chili Cheese Jubilee
Seafood Santa Barbara
Piquant Asparagus
Poppy Sesame Petal Loaf
Super Bundt Cake

Spring   Forks only   *Serves 8*
Clams Orégano
Benne Seed Dip
Veal Milanese
Zucchini Casserole
Salad Continental
Apricot Angel Pie

Elegant   Summer   *Knives and Forks*   *Serves 8*
Shad Roe en Brochette
Brandied Cheese Roll
Rosemary Chicken
Tangerine Rice
Cucumber Mousse
Cheese-filled Strudel

Elegant   Summer   *Knives and Forks*   *Serves 10*
Mushrooms Lenape
Bouchées of Roquefort
Pineapple Prosciutto
Beef in Aspic
Spanish Peas
Pine Nut Bulgur
Herb Pinwheels
Miracle Meringue Torte

Elegant   Summer   *Knives and Forks*   *Serves 12*
Parmesan Olive Appetizers
Baked Camembert
Caviar Mousse
Tenderloin Stuffed with Ham
Tarragon Crab
Baked Crusty Tomatoes
Confetti Rice Salad
Royal Trifle

Stand-up Buffet   Summer   Forks only   Serves 12
Zesty Parmesan Cubes
Danish Cheese Liver Pâté
Pearl of the Sea Mousse
Meatballs Piemonte
Chutney Chicken Salad
California Vegetable Bowl
Italian Crescents
Easy Schnecken
Chocolate Mint Sticks
Frosted Walnut Bars

Elegant   Fall   Knives and Forks   Serves 12
Shrimp in Jackets
Elysian Cheese Mold
Pickled Cocktail Beets
Green Noodles Chicken
Vitello Tonnato
Avocado and Hearts of Palm Salad
Apricot Mousse

Simple   Fall   Stand-up   Forks only   Serves 8
Eggplant Puffs
New England Lobster Mold
Pasta Florentine
Spiked Bean Salad
Garlic Cheese Bread
Bernice's Most Heavenly Hash

Elegant   Fall   Knives and Forks   Serves 12
Ham Nuggets
Dutch Cheese Appetizer
Smoky Egg Dip
Herbed Veal
Chicken Tahitian
Tomato Aspic in Cheese Crust
Savory Butterflake Loaf
Mocha Icebox Cake

Sit-down   Fall   Knives and Forks   Serves 12
Hot Shrimp Toast
Riviera Roquefort Log
Colton Manor Moussaka
Rolled Chicken Breasts
Nutty Rice with Mushrooms
Green Bean Salad
Tia Maria Cold Soufflé

Informal   Fall   Knives and Forks   Serves 8
Deviled Sardines
Crocked Cheese
Sweet and Sour Beef
Broccoli San Vincente
Beer Barrel Potatoes
Orange Spongecake

Cocktails Only

COCKTAIL PARTY FOR 10
Curried Crab Tarts
Ham Tarts
Puffed Cheesies
Aloha Spread
Shrimp and Artichokes Vinaigrette

COCKTAIL PARTY FOR 25
Fanciful Crabmeat Rolls
Ruby Red Franks
Cheese Pinwheels
Hammed-up Mushrooms
Tivoli Clam Dip
Snappy Cheese Apple
Antipasto Crostini

COCKTAIL PARTY FOR 40-*plus* (*lots of napkins and plates is good idea—almost enough for supper*)
Meat-filled Triangles
Sour-Cream Onion Pie
Gourmet Butterfly Shrimp
Chili con Queso
Nantucket Pancakes
Finger Lickin' Spareribs
Nova Scotia Mousse
Pacific Avocado Dip
Eggplant Caviar
Brandied Country Pâté

Hot Hors d'Oeuvres

Baked Camembert

Cut into half lengthwise each wedge in contents of
   4 cans Camembert cheese
Dip into
   4 slightly beaten eggs
Then dip into
   1¼ cups slivered almonds
Press almonds with a flat knife to make sure they stick. Bake at
500° in a buttered pan for 2 to 3 minutes, until cheese begins to
melt. Serve from same pan with
   mild-flavored crackers or dark bread.

Bouchées of Roquefort

#1   makes 15 shells

Mix together thoroughly
   2 ounces Roquefort cheese, crumbled
   1½ teaspoons brandy
   ⅛ teaspoon salt
   dash pepper
   2 tablespoons butter
   1 tablespoon cream cheese
Spoon this mixture into
   15 miniature pastry shells
Refrigerate, if desired. To serve, bring to room temperature and
bake for 5 minutes at 300°.

Cheese Pinwheels

* #3   makes 42

Prepare according to package directions
  ½ package piecrust mix (enough for 1-crust pie)
Roll out into rectangle 6 x 12 inches
Cream until soft
  ⅓ cup butter
  1 cup grated sharp cheese (¼ pound)
Add
  2 teaspoons light cream
  ¼ teaspoon salt
  ⅛ teaspoon paprika
Stir until smooth. Then add
  1 egg white, unbeaten
Mix thoroughly. Spread cheese mixture over dough. Roll up as for jelly roll. Wrap in heavy duty foil and freeze or refrigerate at least overnight. When ready to serve, cut into ¼-inch slices while still slightly chilled, then bring to room temperature. Place on ungreased baking sheet and bake at 425° for 6 to 8 minutes until golden.

Chef's Favorite

#1   makes 48 caps

Rinse and remove stems from
  48 mushrooms
Reserve stems for other use.
Cook
  1 pound well-seasoned sausage meat
long enough to remove most of the fat. Drain and add
  seasoned bread crumbs
enough to bind the mixture. Mix in a
  pinch of sage
Stuff caps with sausage mixture and refrigerate. To serve, bake at 350° until mushrooms have softened and filling is juicy, about 20 minutes. Serve hot.

Chesapeake Clams and Cheese

* # 1 makes 7 cups

Simmer for 15 minutes

4 (7½-ounce) cans minced clams, well drained, reserve juice
4 teaspoons lemon juice

Blend in blender

2 onions, cut up
2 green peppers, cut up
½ cup fresh parsley
enough clam juice to make it spread easily

Add this to simmering clams with

½ pound butter
2 tablespoons orégano

When butter melts, add

4 teaspoons hot pepper sauce
½ teaspoon seasoned pepper
1½ cups bread crumbs

Mix until consistency of oatmeal. Place in pie plate. Refrigerate or freeze. When ready to serve bring to room temperature and cover surface with

slices of American cheese

Sprinkle with

grated Parmesan cheese
paprika

Bake at 325° for 15 to 20 minutes until hot and bubbly. Serve spread on

shredded-wheat wafers.

Chicken Sticks

* #2   makes 30

Cut off and discard bony tips of
>   *3 pounds chicken wings (about 15)*

Divide each wing in half by cutting through joint with a sharp knife. Wash and drain on paper towels.

Melt in a large shallow baking pan
>   *1 cup butter*

Mix together
>   *1½ cups flour*
>   *⅓ cup sesame seeds*
>   *1 tablespoon salt*
>   *½ teaspoon ground ginger*

Roll chicken pieces, one at a time, in butter, then in flour mixture. Set aside on sheets of wax paper. Arrange in single layer, not touching, in same pan. Bake at 350° for 1 hour. Refrigerate or freeze. When ready to serve, bring to room temperature and broil 3 to 5 minutes until golden.

Chili con Queso

#3

Chop
> 1 green pepper
> 2 large onions

Sauté in
> 2 tablespoons butter

until soft. In top of double boiler, heat
> 1 can cream of tomato soup, undiluted

Add and allow to melt
> 1 cup grated very sharp Cheddar cheese

Add the green pepper and onion with
> 2 to 3 tablespoons chili powder
> Worchestershire sauce to taste

Serve hot (or refrigerate and reheat to serve) with
> corn chips or tortilla chips.

Clams Orégano

* #1   makes 36

Combine
> ¼ pound butter
> 4 cloves garlic, mashed
> ¼ cup fine bread crumbs
> 1 teaspoon orégano
> few dashes hot pepper sauce
> 1 teaspoon chopped parsley
> 2 tablespoons minced onion

Place one teaspoon of this mixture on top of each of
> 3 dozen littleneck or cherrystone clams on half shell

Refrigerate or freeze. When ready to serve, bake at 375° for 10 minutes, then brown under broiler.

Crabby Mushrooms

#1   makes 24

Flake
> ½ *pound crabmeat*

Mix well with
> ¼ *cup mayonnaise*
> ⅓ *cup finely chopped black olives*
> 2 *tablespoons chopped parsley*
> ¼ *teaspoon garlic powder*
> ¼ *teaspoon onion powder*

Wash and stem
> 24 *large mushrooms*

Stuff mushrooms with crab mixture. Sprinkle with
> *grated American cheese*

Place in shallow pan with enough water to cover bottom of pan. Bake at 400° for 12 to 15 minutes. Remove from liquid and refrigerate. When ready to serve, reheat for 5 to 10 minutes at 350°.

Curried Crab Tarts

#1   makes 48

Combine
> 1 *tablespoon flour*
> 1½ *teaspoons curry powder*

Slowly add
> 1½ *cups hot milk*

Stir to keep smooth. Then stir in
> 3 *cups flaked crabmeat, picked over to remove any shell*

Cook over low heat for 2 to 3 minutes. Add
> *dash hot pepper sauce*

Use this mixture to fill
> 48 *packaged tiny fluted tart shells*

Filling may be made ahead, but fill tart shells just before serving. Heat at 450° for 5 to 6 minutes.

Deviled Sardines

1   makes 16

Lightly toast
    4 slices white bread
Cover toast with contents of
    2 (4-ounce) cans sardines, drained
Combine and spread sardines with
    1 teaspoon prepared mustard
    1 teaspoon bottled cocktail sauce
    1 tablespoon grated Parmesan cheese
    2 tablespoons melted butter
When ready to serve, place under broiler until brown and cut into canapé-sized pieces.

Eggplant Puffs

* # 1   makes 42

Cook in boiling water until tender (15 to 20 minutes)
    1 medium eggplant, whole
Peel and mash pulp with a fork. Add
    ½ cup grated Swiss cheese
    1 egg, slightly beaten
    3 to 4 tablespoons bread crumbs
    ½ teaspoon ground cumin
    ½ teaspoon garlic powder
    ½ teaspoon lemon juice
    ½ teaspoon salt
    ¼ teaspoon pepper

Beat well. Shape into small balls and refrigerate at least 1 hour.
Roll balls in
> *flour*

Fry until crisp in deep fat. Refrigerate or freeze. To serve, bring
to room temperature and heat at 350° for 15 minutes.

Fanciful Crabmeat Rolls

#1   makes 20

Partially cook, not browning
> 10 *slices bacon, cut in half*

Drain on absorbent paper and set aside. In a bowl place
> ½ *cup fine bread crumbs*
> ½ *pound crabmeat, flaked*
> ¼ *cup finely chopped parsley*
> 1 *egg*
> 2 *tablespoons tomato sauce*
> 1 *tablespoon lemon juice*
> ¼ *teaspoon salt*
> ¼ *teaspoon Worcestershire sauce*
> *dash pepper*

Mix well. Wrap a half slice bacon around 1 tablespoon of this
mixture and secure with toothpick. Refrigerate, if desired. To
serve, return to room temperature and place on broiler rack about
5 inches from heat. Broil 10 to 15 minutes, turning several times
to brown rolls evenly.

Finger Lickin' Spareribs

\#1 makes 72

Just serve lots of napkins. They go so fast!
Combine and simmer for 15 minutes

>   *1 cup white vinegar*
>   *1 clove garlic, crushed*
>   *1 tablespoon olive oil*
>   *2½ tablespoons Worcestershire sauce*
>   *dash hot pepper sauce*
>   *1 tablespoon sugar*
>   *⅓ cup catsup*
>   *1 teaspoon dry mustard*
>   *1 teaspoon salt*
>   *½ teaspoon pepper*
>   *½ teaspoon paprika*
>   *1 tablespoon soy sauce*
>   *2 jars strained baby food fruit—peaches, pears or apricots*

Pour this marinade over

>   *12 pounds spareribs, cut into individual pieces*

Marinate overnight. Pour off juice and use to baste while baking at 400° for ½ hour. At this point, they may be refrigerated or frozen. When ready to serve, bring to room temperature and place under broiler until brown and crisp.

Gourmet Butterfly Shrimp

\#1 makes about 24

Remove shell partially from

>   *1 pound raw shrimp, leaving shell intact on tail piece*

Be sure not to break off tail meat. With a sharp knife, slit along the back and wash away the black vein. Split the shrimp lengthwise not quite to the end and put the halves back together with mixture of

¼ *pound Roquefort cheese*
½ *cup whipped cream cheese*
Beat together
    1 *egg*
    1 *tablespoon water*
Mix together
    ⅓ *cup fine bread crumbs*
    ¼ *cup flour*
    2 *tablespoons paprika*
    few grains cayenne
Dip each shrimp in egg, then roll in crumb mixture. Fry about 3 minutes or until golden in deep fat heated to 350°. Drain on paper towels. Refrigerate or freeze. To serve, return to room temperature and bake at 350° for 10 minutes.

Ham and Pineapple Savories

#2   makes about 30

Heat
    2 *tablespoons butter*
    ¼ to ½ *teaspoon curry powder*
Add to butter and cook until vegetables are softened
    2 *tablespoons finely chopped green onion*
    ¼ *cup finely chopped celery*
    1 *cup finely chopped cooked ham*
Remove from heat and stir in
    ⅛ *teaspoon dry mustard*
    3 *tablespoons mayonnaise*
    1 *(8½-ounce) can crushed pineapple, drained*
Spoon into
    1 *package of 30 minature fluted patty shells*
Bake at 350° just long enough to heat through, about 7 to 10 minutes. The ham-pineapple mixture may be made in advance and refrigerated. Do not fill the shells more than a couple of hours before serving.

Ham Nuggets

*#2 makes 24

Blend together
    1 cup grated Cheddar cheese
    ¼ cup butter
    1 tablespoon Worcestershire sauce
Add
    ¾ cup flour
    ½ teaspoon paprika
Mix until a dough is formed. Mold 2 to 3 teaspoons of dough around
    1-inch cubes of boiled or baked ham
Enclose ham entirely. Chill until firm, or freeze. When ready to serve, bring to room temperature and bake at 400° for 10 to 15 minutes. Serve hot.

Ham Tarts

#1 makes 48

Soften
    ¾ cup butter
Mix with
    1½ teaspoons prepared mustard
Stir in
    3 cups ground cooked ham
    ¾ green pepper, finely chopped
    2 tablespoons minced onion
Use to fill
    48 packaged tiny fluted tart shells
Filling may be made ahead, but fill tart shells just before serving. Heat at 450° for 5 to 6 minutes.

Hammed-up Mushrooms

 #1   makes 48

Wash and remove stems from
   4 dozen medium-sized mushrooms
Sauté caps in
   3 tablespoons butter
Make mixture of
   2 cups ground ham
   ½ cup sour cream
   ½ teaspoon salt
   ¼ teaspoon pepper
Stuff caps and refrigerate. When ready to serve, sprinkle with
   bread crumbs
Heat at 350° for 10 minutes.

Hot Frijole Chip Dip

#3

Over low heat warm
   2 (11-ounce) cans chili beef soup
   2 tablespoons red wine or sherry
Blend in
   ½ cup minced onion
   ½ cup diced green pepper
   1 (2-ounce) bottle stuffed olives, sliced
   1 teaspoon chili powder
   ½ teaspoon cumin
Stir until mixture bubbles. Add a handful at a time
   1 cup shredded aged Cheddar cheese
Wait between additions until cheese melts. Refrigerate if desired.
When ready to serve, reheat slowly, then pour into warm chafing
dish. Sprinkle on

    ¼ cup shredded aged Cheddar cheese
Keep hot while serving with
    potato chips and corn chips.

Hot Pizza Dip

*

For emergencies.
Combine and heat
    1 (8-ounce) package cream cheese, softened
    1 can pizza sauce with meat or sausage
    Parmesan cheese
Serve with
    corn chips.

Hot Shrimp Toast

*   makes 60

A favorite Chinese dish.
Grind together to a paste with finest blade of meat grinder or
blend in an electric blender
    1 pound raw shrimp, shelled and deveined
    1 (5-ounce) can water chestnuts, drained
    ¼ cup chopped green onions, green part only
Add
    2 teaspoons salt
    1 teaspoon sugar
    1 beaten egg
Spread mixture on
    15 slices thin sliced white bread

Sprinkle lightly with
    fine dry bread crumbs
Cut each slice into four triangles. Heat oil in a frying pan so that
oil is 1 inch deep and very hot. Fry each triangle shrimp side down
first, then brown on other side, about 2 minutes each side. Drain
on absorbent paper. Freeze. When ready to serve, defrost and
reheat in 400° oven for 5 minutes.

Meat-filled Triangles

*   makes about 80

*These are made with phyllo (a layered dough of Greek origin) or
strudel dough and are known in Greek as Kreatopitakia.*
Sauté
    1 small onion, finely chopped
in
    1 tablespoon hot olive oil
Add and brown well
    ¾ pound ground chuck
    ¼ pound ground pork
Drain off all fat. Combine and add to meat
    ¼ cup dry red wine
    2 tablespoons tomato sauce
    ¼ cup water
Cover and simmer for 30 minutes. Remove from heat; add
    1 egg, slightly beaten
    ½ cup grated Parmesan cheese
    2 tablespoons bread crumbs
Blend well. Cool the mixture.
If it has been frozen, defrost according to package directions
    1 pound phyllo or strudel dough
Remove sheets from box. Keep the sections covered with a damp
cloth and place on a damp towel to prevent drying out. Cut sheets
into three or four sections, lengthwise. They should be about 3½

inches wide. Work quickly so dough does not dry out. Fold over about 1 inch at the bottom of a single strip and brush with some of

¾ to 1 pound melted butter

A small paint brush bought for this purpose works better than a pastry brush. Using a teaspoon of filling, place it at the folded end. Then fold up strip to make triangular shape. Fold as you fold an American flag. When a strip is completely folded, its shape is that of a triangle. Place all the triangles on cookie sheets and brush with

melted butter

Bake at 325° for 35 minutes or until lightly browned. If desired, cool and freeze. To serve, reheat frozen at 325° for about 10 minutes, or until puffed again and piping hot. If you do not freeze, then serve immediately after baking.

Mushrooms Lenape

#2   makes 30 shells

A *favorite of the mushroom country in Pennsylvania.*
In skillet sauté
½ cup minced onion
in
2 tablespoons butter or margarine
until soft and just beginning to brown.
Drain well, reserving broth from
2 (6-ounce) cans chopped broiled-in-butter mushrooms
Add mushrooms and
½ clove garlic, minced
½ teaspoon marjoram
to skillet and cook until mushrooms start to brown. Combine
½ cup mushroom broth
1 tablespoon cornstarch
1 teaspoon bottled gravy enricher

Add to skillet and cook, stirring, until sauce thickens. Remove
from heat and stir in
   ½ cup sour cream
Use to fill
   1 package miniature prebaked pastry shells
and heat at 350°.

Mushrooms Stuffed with Anchovies

#2   makes 24

Sauté for 2 to 3 minutes
   24 medium mushroom caps
in
   3 tablespoons olive oil
Mix together
   1 (2½-ounce) can anchovy fillets, drained and chopped
   1 clove garlic, mashed
   1 teaspoon lemon juice
   ¾ cup bread crumbs
   ¼ cup chopped parsley
   pepper to taste
Fill caps with mixture. Drizzle over them
   1 tablespoon olive oil
Refrigerate. When ready to serve, bake at 350° until hot, about
15 minutes.

Nantucket Pancakes

#1   makes about 3 dozen 2½-inch pancakes

Following directions on package of pancake mix make
   batter for 12 regular-sized pancakes

but substitute for half the milk in the recipe an equal amount of
   clam juice from 2 (7½-ounce) cans minced clams
Add
   pinch cayenne
Then add
   more milk
to make a very thin batter. Stir in the
   drained clams
   2 tablespoons chopped chives
Refrigerate batter overnight to "ripen." To serve, stir batter, add
more milk to thin, if necessary. Put a heaping teaspoonful of batter on greased, heated skillet and brown on first side. Turn and
brown on second side. Keep warm on hot tray.

Nippy Nibbles

#1   makes 24

Stuff
   24 pitted ripe olives
with
   24 cubes sharp Cheddar cheese
Wrap each with
   2-inch strip bacon
Fasten with toothpick. When ready to serve, broil until bacon is
crisp. Drain on absorbent paper.

Onion Cheese Wafers

*#3   makes 60

Mix together thoroughly
   ½ cup butter
   ½ pound Cheddar cheese, grated

Blend in
    ½ *teaspoon salt*
    1 *cup flour*
    ½ *package* (2 *tablespoons*) *dry onion soup mix*
Shape into two or three rolls, 1 inch in diameter. Wrap in wax
paper. Refrigerate or freeze. When ready to serve, slice roll into
¼-inch-thick slices and bake on ungreased cookie sheet 10 to 12
minutes at 375°.

Oriental Shrimp

#1   makes 48

Marinate 4 hours or overnight
    2 *pounds raw shrimp, shelled and deveined*
in mixture of
    ⅔ *cup soy sauce*
    ½ *cup peanut oil*
    2 *tablespoons brown sugar*
    1½ *teaspoons ground ginger*
    6 *scallions, minced*
When ready to serve, drain shrimp. Skewer them and let guests
grill their own over cocktail-sized hibachi. If desired, the hostess
may grill them all in advance and serve them warm from a chafing
dish.

Parmesan Olive Appetizers

*#   makes 24

Separate dough from
    1 *can refrigerated crescent rolls*
into 8 triangles. Roll each out and cut into 3 smaller triangles.

Dip dough on one side into
    ½ cup grated Parmesan cheese
Place
    1 large stuffed olive (24 total)
in center of each triangle on top of cheese. Roll up. Place on
greased cookie sheet and bake at 375° 5 to 6 minutes. Refrigerate
or freeze. When ready to serve, return to room temperature and
bake at 375° for 6 to 7 minutes more, until golden.

Puffed Cheesies

#3   makes 42

Knead together
    1½ cups grated Swiss cheese
    ½ cup grated Parmesan cheese
    ½ cup butter at room temperature
    ¾ cup flour
    ¾ teaspoon salt
    ⅛ teaspoon cayenne
    ⅛ teaspoon nutmeg
Form into ball and chill at least 15 minutes. Break off tablespoon-
fuls and form each into ball, then flatten into circle about ¼ inch
thick. Arrange on baking sheet, leaving space between. Brush tops
with
    1 egg beaten with 1 teaspoon water
Sprinkle with
    ½ cup grated Swiss cheese
Refrigerate. When ready to serve, bake at 425° for 10 minutes
until puffed and lightly browned.

Quiche Pâté

* # 1   serves 16

This is one of the most marvelous hors d'oeuvres or additions to a buffet table imaginable. It combines two super ideas in foods, and the wedding is even better than each alone.

Separate
>   1 egg

Place yolk in large bowl along with
>   *4 whole eggs*

Beat white and brush over bottom and sides of
>   *2 (9-inch) unbaked pie shells*

Combine
>   *1¾ pounds canned liver pâté*
>   *½ cup chopped onion*
>   *4 cloves garlic, crushed*
>   *½ cup packaged dry bread crumbs*
>   *½ teaspoon nutmeg*

Mix well and spoon into prepared pie shells, spreading evenly.
In
>   *2 tablespoons hot butter*

sauté for 2 minutes or until lightly golden
>   *¼ cup chopped onion*

Beat with eggs
>   *2 cups heavy cream*
>   *½ teaspoon salt*
>   *dash cayenne*
>   *dash nutmeg*

Stir in sautéed onion and
>   *⅔ cup grated Parmesan cheese*
>   *¼ cup dry sherry*

Pour half of this mixture over each pie shell. Freeze or refrigerate. When ready to serve return to room temperature and bake 30 to 40 minutes at 375° or until knife inserted 1 inch from edge comes out clean. Let cool on wire rack about 1 hour. Serve warm in very small wedges.

Quick Cheese Onion Pie

3   makes 2 9-inch pies

Unroll and separate dough into 16 triangles from
   2 cans refrigerated crescent rolls
Place in 2 9 x 9-inch-square baking pans, pressing pieces down
and together to form crust. Combine
   4 eggs, beaten
   4 cups light cream
   1½ teaspoons salt
   2 teaspoons Worcestershire sauce
Stir in
   3½ cups shredded Swiss cheese
Sprinkle over crusts contents of
   1 (3½-ounce) can French-fried onion rings
Pour egg mixture into crusts. Sprinkle with
   18 slices cooked, crumbled bacon
   1 (3½-ounce) can French-fried onion rings
Bake at 325° for 30 to 40 minutes. Allow to cool 5 minutes before
cutting.

Ruby Red Franks

* # 2

In saucepan combine
   1 (1-pound, 5-ounce) can cherry pie filling
   1 cup rosé or dry red wine
Heat slowly and add
   1 (1-pound) package cocktail franks
When ready to serve, heat through and serve with picks from
chafing dish.

Shad Roe en Brochette

#1

Drain liquid from
>   2 cans shad roe

Cut the roe into small squares, about ¼ inch. Wrap each square in
>   small strip of bacon

Secure with a pick. When ready to serve, broil until bacon is crisp. Serve hot.

Shrimp in Jackets

* #1   makes 28

Cook, shell, and devein
>   2 pounds shrimp

Sprinkle shrimp lightly with
>   lime juice
>   dash cayenne

Mix together for batter
>   ¾ cup flour
>   ½ cup yellow corn meal
>   1 teaspoon salt
>   2 teaspoons baking powder
>   1 egg, beaten
>   ¾ cup milk
>   ¼ cup water

Dip shrimp in batter, then fry in deep fat, 375°, until golden brown. Drain on absorbent paper. Refrigerate or freeze. To serve, defrost and reheat in 550° oven for 10 minutes. Serve with
>   mustard-flavored mayonnaise (available commercially, or make your own, using 1 part prepared mustard to three parts mayonnaise).

Sour-Cream Onion Pie

* # 1

Line an 8 x 8-inch-square pan with
   pastry for a 9-inch pie
Prick well with fork. Bake at 450° for about 10 minutes or until
pastry is lightly browned. Meanwhile sauté
   2¼ cups thinly sliced onions
in
   4 tablespoons butter or margarine
for 15 minutes, stirring frequently. Blend in
   2 tablespoons flour
Add
   ⅓ cup dry sherry
Cook, stirring for a minute or so. Add
   1 pint sour cream
   3 eggs, slightly beaten
   1 teaspoon Worcestershire sauce
   ½ teaspoon paprika
   salt and pepper to taste
Blend well. Pour into baked crust. Refrigerate or freeze. When
ready to serve, return to room temperature and bake at 350°
for 40 minutes or until firm and golden. Remove from oven and
let stand 10 minutes before cutting into squares and serving.

South-of-the-Border Dip

* #3

Combine in top of double boiler
>   2 *cups cooked or canned red, pink or pinto beans, sieved or*
>   *mashed smooth*
>   ¼ *pound butter*
>   ¼ *pound thin sliced provolone cheese*
>   4 *canned jalapeño peppers,* chopped very fine*
>   1 *teaspoon jalapeño juice*
>   2 *tablespoons minced onion*
>   1 *clove garlic, crushed*

Stir occasionally and heat until cheese is melted and mixture is hot. Refrigerate. To serve, reheat and serve hot from chafing dish or food warmer with
>   *corn chips or tortilla chips.*

* If unavailable, substitute any other hot pepper, canned or pickled.

Spinach Cheese Rolls

*   makes about 40 pieces

These are made with phyllo (a flaky dough of Greek origin) or strudel dough.
In
>   ¼ *cup olive oil*

sauté for 5 minutes
>   1 *medium onion, finely chopped*

Add
>   1 (10-ounce) *package frozen chopped spinach, defrosted and*
>   *thoroughly drained*

Simmer until most of the moisture has evaporated.
Crumble into small pieces
>   ½ *pound feta cheese*

Combine and blend well with
   6 ounces pot cheese
Add and mix well
   3 eggs, well beaten
Toss into spinach-onion mixture
   ¼ cup bread crumbs
Then combine with cheese mixture. Blend well.
Defrost according to package directions (if it has been frozen)
   ½ pound phyllo or strudel dough
Remove sheets from box. Keep the sections covered with damp
cloth and place on a damp towel to prevent drying out. Cut sheets
into four quarters. Work quickly so dough does not dry out.
Brush each sheet with some of
   ½ cup melted butter
Place 1 tablespoon of filling 1 inch from edge of bottom of sheet.
Fold the inch margin over mixture; fold long side edges in, overlapping, and roll completely to end.
Use a new 1½- to 2-inch paintbrush for brushing on butter. Place
rolls on cookie sheets. Brush tops with butter and bake at 425°
for 20 minutes or until lightly browned. Serve warm. Or cool and
freeze. To serve, reheat, frozen, at 325° for about 10 minutes to
heat through.

Vienna Pinwheels

*#2   makes 48

Mix together as for pie crust, by cutting in shortening with fork
   1 cup flour
   ¼ teaspoon salt
   ½ cup butter
   4 ounces cream cheese
Roll out paper thin on a floured board. Spread with mixture of
   ½ pound soft liverwurst
   1 teaspoon lemon juice

Roll up dough as for jelly roll and wrap in wax paper. Refrigerate
or freeze. When ready to serve, defrost and cut into thin slices.
Bake at 450° for 10 to 12 minutes.

Wurst-stuffed Mushrooms

#2   makes 24

Wash and dry, remove stems from
  1 pound mushrooms
Turn stem side up, brush with
  4 tablespoons melted butter
Broil lightly. Fill with mixture of the following:
  ¼ pound soft liverwurst
  1 tablespoon Worcestershire sauce
  1 tablespoon mayonnaise
  1 tablespoon onion salt
Top caps with mixture of
  3 tablespoons bread crumbs
  2 tablespoons grated Parmesan cheese
Refrigerate. When ready to serve, broil 3 to 5 minutes until
brown.

Zesty Parmesan Crisps

*#2   makes 64

Remove crusts from
  8 slices white bread
Cut each slice into 8 sticks (easier to do when slightly frozen).
Place on baking sheet and toast at 400° for 5 minutes. Meanwhile in shallow dish combine
  1½ cups grated Parmesan cheese

1¼ *teaspoons chili powder*

Into another dish pour

1 *cup melted butter or margarine*

Roll each stick first in butter, then in cheese mixture. Refrigerate or freeze. To serve, place sticks on baking sheet and bake at 400° for about 5 minutes until golden brown. Serve warm.

Cold Hors d'Oeuvres

Aloha Spread

#3   makes 2 cups

Sharp, tangy, and sweet.
Blend together
  1 (8-ounce) package cream cheese, softened
  3 ounces blue cheese, crumbled
Stir in
  ⅓ cup drained crushed pineapple
  ⅓ cup chopped pecans (if serving same day)
  ½ teaspoon ground ginger
Mix well and chill. To serve garnish with
  sprigs of parsley
  pimiento
Spread on
  crackers
If making in advance, add pecans just a few hours before serving
so they will remain crunchy.

Antipasto Crostini

#2   makes 1 pint

A chicken liver pâté with a difference.
Sauté until transparent
  ½ cup minced onion

in
   4 tablespoons butter
Stir in
   1 (10½-ounce) can chicken broth
Cook over medium heat until almost evaporated. Add
   1 pound chicken livers
Cook over low heat for 5 minutes, stirring. Add
   ¼ teaspoon freshly ground pepper
   1 tablespoon drained chopped capers
Cook until livers are done. Mash while warm or blend in blender.
Refrigerate. When ready to serve, bring to room temperature and
serve with
   crackers, rye rounds, Italian bread.

Barbecue Cheese Dip

*

For emergencies or otherwise.
Combine all ingredients, using the barbecue sauce to your taste
   1 (8-ounce) package cream cheese, softened
   barbecue sauce with onion
   2 teaspoons minced onion
   1 teaspoon Worcestershire sauce
   1 tablespoon grated Parmesan cheese
Serve with
   chips or crackers.

Basic Black and Gold

#3   makes 2 cups basic mixture

This can be served hot or cold, as a dip, spread, or in balls.
Cut in coarse pieces
   1 cup ripe olives

Combine olives with
>8 ounces sharp Cheddar cheese, finely grated
>¼ cup mayonnaise
>2 tablespoons finely chopped onion
>1 teaspoon curry powder
>½ teaspoon garlic salt

Mix well.

HOT: Spread on toast rounds and broil until cheese melts.

CHILLED: Form balls from teaspoon of mixture. Roll in chopped parsley, sesame seeds or chili powder.

Chill and serve with melba toast.

DIP: Mix equal parts of mixture with sour cream.

Serve with crackers or chips.

Benne Seed Dip

#3   makes 2½ cups

Sauté until lightly browned
>2 ounces sesame seeds

in
>1 tablespoon butter

Remove from heat and add
>¼ cup grated Parmesan cheese

Blend until smooth
>1 cup sour cream
>½ cup mayonnaise
>1 tablespoon tarragon vinegar

Add
>1 tablespoon sugar
>1 teaspoon salt
>1 clove garlic, mashed
>¼ cup minced green pepper
>¼ cup minced cucumber
>2 tablespoons minced onion
>sesame seed mixture

Serve with
>chips or crackers.

Black Olive Dip

#3

Combine and refrigerate at least 1 hour
>   *2 cups chopped ripe olives*
>   *2 tablespoons minced onion*
>   *dash cayenne pepper*
>   *2 diced pimientos*
>   *garlic powder to taste*
>   *½ teaspoon lemon juice*
>   *1 pint sour cream*

Use for dippers
>   *corn chips, potato chips or crackers.*

Brandied Cheese Roll

#3   makes 2 rolls

Beat until creamy with electric beater
>   *¾ pound Roquefort cheese at room temperature*

Add
>   *½ pound cream cheese at room temperature*

Continue beating until creamy. Add
>   *¼ pound sweet butter*
>   *3 tablespoons brandy*

Chill until firm enough to shape into 2 rolls. Then roll in
>   *finely chopped pecans or walnuts.*

This tastes better if made a few days ahead. Use as spread with crackers or spread on cocktail rye or melba toast and pop under broiler.

Brandied Country Pâté

#3   one 9 x 5 x 3 loaf

Fantastic flavor!

Sauté lightly
> *½ pound chicken livers*

in
> *4 tablespoons butter*

Put them through the fine blade of the meat grinder with
> *2 eggs*
> *1 onion*
> *2 cloves garlic*

Combine this mixture with
> *½ cup brandy*
> *½ teaspoon allspice*
> *1 tablespoon salt*
> *1 teaspoon rosemary*
> *½ teaspoon freshly ground pepper*
> *1 pound mildly seasoned ground sausage*
> *¼ cup flour*

Line a bread pan with
> *strips of salt pork*

Pour pâté mixture into mold and cover with a lid or aluminum foil. Bake at 350° for 1½ to 2 hours or until liquid in pan and fat are clear. Cool for 15 minutes. Pour off fat. Weight pâté with a brick or other heavy object and cool completely in refrigerator. To serve, unmold, remove excess fat. Decorate top with
> *black olive pieces*
> *strips of pimiento*

Serve with
> *mildly flavored crackers or water biscuits.*

Caviar Mousse

#2   fills 1½-quart mold

Combine
>   6 ounces red caviar
>   ¼ cup finely chopped parsley
>   1 tablespoon grated onion
>   1 teaspoon grated lemon peel

Stir in
>   1 pint sour cream

Whip until stiff
>   1 cup heavy cream

Sprinkle
>   1 envelope unflavored gelatin

over
>   ¼ cup water

Cook over low heat, stirring, until gelatin is dissolved. Stir gelatin into caviar and sour cream mixture. Fold in whipped cream and add
>   1 clove garlic, mashed
>   ½ teaspoon pepper

Chill in 1½-quart fish-shaped mold until set. Unmold and serve with
>   small squares of thin pumpernickel spread with sweet butter.

Ceci Rémoulade

#3

Drain and rinse in cold water
>   1 (1-pound, 4-ounce) can chick peas (garbanzos)

Chop together
>   2 anchovy fillets
>   1 clove garlic, finely minced

Blend with chick peas and
> 1 tablespoon chopped capers
> 1 teaspoon finely chopped green onions
> 2 tablespoons finely chopped parsley
> salt and freshly ground black pepper
> lemon juice to taste

Add just enough to bind of
> ¼ to ½ cup mayonnaise

Chill.
Serve this hors d'oeuvre with plate and fork.

Cheese 'n' Chutney

#2   makes 36

Mix together
> ¼ pound blue cheese
> ½ pound cream cheese
> ¼ cup chopped chutney

Form into small balls. Roll balls in
> 6 ounces chopped toasted almonds.

Cheese Sticks

*#3   makes 24

Mix together thoroughly
> 1 (5-ounce) jar Old English Cheese spread
> ½ cup butter
> 1 cup plus 1 tablespoon flour

Add
> 1 tablespoon caraway seeds
> ½ teaspoon Worcestershire sauce

Squirt with flat pastry tube to make 3-inch bars. Bake 10 to 12
minutes at 375°. Store in airtight container or freeze.

Chicken Nut Pinwheels

#2   makes 36

Remove crusts from
    1 loaf sliced white bread
Roll each slice thin with a rolling pin. Spread slices with mixture
of
    ¼ pound butter
    1 teaspoon lemon juice
Grind together
    2 cups diced cooked chicken
    1 cup diced roasted almonds
    1 cup diced celery
Add
    1 cup mayonnaise
    1 teaspoon salt
    dash seasoned pepper
Spread bread with filling and roll tightly as for jelly roll. Wrap rolls
in damp cloth and wax paper. Chill. Slice each roll in half to
serve.

Chutney Olive Dip

#3

Combine and chill
    2 cups sour cream
    ½ cup chopped chutney
    ½ cup chopped black olives
    1½ teaspoons minced onion
    ¾ teaspoon salad seasoning
    ¼ teaspoon curry powder
Serve with
    chips or crackers.

Crocked Cheese

* # 7

In large bowl blend thoroughly
   3 (5-ounce) jars Old English cheese
   1 (8-ounce) package cream cheese, softened
   5 ounces blue cheese, softened
   ¼ pound butter, softened
Mix in
   ¾ cup chopped ripe olives
   1 teaspoon grated onion
   1 teaspoon soy sauce
   4 tablespoons gin
Place in cheese crock or serving dish. Cover well and chill at least
overnight. Serve with an assortment of
   crackers.

Danish Cheese Liver Pâté

* # 3

Into a bowl crumble
   8 ounces blue cheese
Add
   4 ounces cream cheese
   1 (4¾-ounce) can liver pâté
Cream well and add, blending
   4 tablespoons brandy
Use as a spread or to fill
   miniature patty shells.

Down East Sardine Mold

#2   fills 1½-quart mold

Drain and mash
>   2 (3¾-ounce) cans skinless and boneless sardines

Coarsely chop
>   3 hard-cooked eggs
>   3 hard-cooked yolks

Combine above with
>   salt and pepper
>   2½ teaspoons prepared mustard
>   6 tablespoons mayonnaise

Mash well. Dissolve
>   1 envelope unflavored gelatin

in
>   2 tablespoons water

and heat to dissolve.
Combine gelatin mixture with above. Pour into greased 1½-quart
mold. Chill. Coarsely chop
>   3 hard-cooked egg whites

Add
>   salt and pepper
>   1 tablespoon capers
>   pinch orégano
>   ¼ teaspoon minced onion
>   dash cayenne
>   ¼ cup mayonnaise
>   ½ cup sour cream

Dissolve
>   1 envelope unflavored gelatin

in
>   2 tablespoons water

Heat to dissolve. Combine gelatin mixture with above ingredients and pour over top of first layer. Chill overnight. To serve,
unmold and serve with
>   crackers.

Dutch Cheese Appetizer

* # 3

Slice an inch from the top of
>   1 *whole Edam cheese* (1¾ *pounds*)

Remove the cheese from the top piece and scoop out the entire cheese, leaving a ½ inch thick shell. Grate the cheese and mix it with
>   1 *cup beer*
>   ¼ *cup soft butter*
>   1 *teaspoon caraway seed*
>   1 *teaspoon dry mustard*
>   ½ *teaspoon celery salt*

Fill cheese with mixture and refrigerate or freeze. When ready to serve, bring to room temperature. Serve with
>   *party rye.*

Eddie Gallaher's Steak Tartare

serves 8

Eddie is one of Washington's foremost radio and TV stars. His avocation is cooking.

Don't make this far ahead as the meat discolors.

With a fork beat
>   2 *eggs*

Add
>   1 *to* 1½ *teaspoons Dijon mustard*
>   *enough salad oil to make mixture consistency of thick egg yolk*

Add
>   1¼ *pounds freshly twice-ground top round, all fat removed*
>   3 *heaping tablespoons chopped onion*
>   *parsley to taste*
>   1 *generous tablespoon capers*

Mix well and add
     2 tablespoons red wine vinegar
Season with
     salt
Shape into loaf and decorate by making diagonal lines with knife
to achieve diamond pattern. Serve with
     thinly sliced black bread.

Eggplant Caviar

*#3   makes 1 quart

The poor man's caviar.
Combine in a large skillet
     1 small eggplant, unpeeled but chopped rather fine
     1 medium onion, coarsely chopped
     ⅓ cup chopped green pepper
     1 (4-ounce) can mushrooms, drained and chopped
     2 cloves garlic, crushed
     ⅓ cup salad oil
Cover pan and simmer for 10 minutes. Add
     1 teaspoon salt
     ½ teaspoon pepper
     ½ teaspoon orégano
     1½ teaspoons sugar
     1 (6-ounce) can tomato paste
     ¼ cup water
     2 tablespoons wine vinegar
     ½ cup chopped stuffed olives
     3 tablespoons pine nuts (pignoli)
     ¼ cup capers
Mix and simmer, covered, for 25 minutes until eggplant is cooked
but not mushy. Chill at least overnight, or freeze. To serve, bring
to room temperature. Serve with
     corn chips.

Elysian Cheese Mold

#2   fills 4-cup mold

Combine and blend
    6 ounces cream cheese, softened
    ½ cup Roquefort cheese
Add
    1 teaspoon Worcestershire sauce
    ¼ cup chopped parsley
    ½ teaspoon salt
    1 teaspoon paprika
Soften
    1 envelope unflavored gelatin
in
    ⅛ cup cold water
Add
    ½ cup hot water
Stir until gelatin is dissolved. Add cheeses and chill until jelly-like (about 1 hour). Fold in
    1 cup heavy cream, whipped
Spoon into 4-cup oiled mold and refrigerate until firm. Serve with *crackers, melba rounds or party rye.*

Green Goddess Dip

#1   2 cups

Combine, cover and chill
    1 medium avocado, mashed with fork
    ½ cup sour cream
    ½ cup mayonnaise
    ⅔ cup chopped ripe olives
    2-ounce can anchovies, mashed
    1 clove garlic, mashed
    1 teaspoon salt
Serve with
    corn chips.

Molded Guacamole

 # 2   fills 1½-quart mold

Because of the gelatin, this guacamole can be made in advance.
Combine and let stand at least 10 minutes
>   1 tablespoon instant minced onion
>   ⅓ cup pale dry sherry

Soften
>   1 envelope unflavored gelatin

in
>   ½ cup cold water

and dissolve completely over low heat. Cool to room temperature. Cut in half, seed, skin and mash coarsely
>   2 large avocados*

Stir in
>   cooled gelatin
>   onion and sherry
>   ⅓ cup sour cream
>   4 teaspoons lemon juice
>   1¼ teaspoons salt
>   ¼ teaspoon hot pepper sauce

Turn into 3-cup mold and chill until firm. Unmold to serve.
Serve with
>   corn chips.

* You can substitute 2 cans frozen guacamole and eliminate the
lemon juice, salt and hot pepper sauce.

New England Lobster Mold

#2   fills 1½-quart mold

Heat
    1 (10½-ounce) can condensed tomato soup (undiluted)
and in it thoroughly blend
    1 (8-ounce) package cream cheese
Soften
    2 envelopes unflavored gelatin
in
    ¼ cup cold water
Dissolve gelatin in hot soup mixture. Cool. Add
    1 cup mayonnaise
    ¾ cup finely chopped celery
    1 large onion, finely chopped
    1 pound lobster meat
    1 teaspoon salt
    ½ teaspoon paprika
    2 dashes hot pepper sauce
    1 teaspoon Worcestershire sauce
    2 teaspoons prepared white horseradish
Place in lightly greased 1½-quart fish-shaped mold and chill until
firm. Unmold and serve with
    crackers or party rye.

Nova Scotia Mousse

#2   fills 1½-quart mold

Sprinkle
    1 envelope unflavored gelatin
onto
    ¼ cup cold water

Dissolve gelatin thoroughly in
>   *½ cup hot light cream*

Cool. Mash together until smooth
>   *8 ounces cream cheese, softened*
>   *1 cup sour cream*
>   *1 teaspoon Worcestershire sauce*
>   *¼ teaspoon hot pepper sauce*
>   *1 clove garlic, mashed*
>   *2 tablespoons chopped chives*

Stir into dissolved gelatin. Add
>   *1 teaspoon lemon juice*
>   *1 tablespoon chopped parsley*
>   *1 tablespoon prepared white horseradish*
>   *½ pound Nova Scotia salmon, coarsely chopped*
>   *½ cup chopped black olives*

Fold in carefully
>   *4 ounces red caviar*

Pour into well-greased, 3-cup, fish-shaped mold. Refrigerate until firm. Unmold and serve with
>   *party rye.*

Pacific Avocado Dip

#1   makes 2 cups

Mash with a fork
>   *1 large avocado*

Add and blend thoroughly
>   *½ cup cottage cheese*

Then add
>   *½ cup chopped green olives*
>   *½ cup chili sauce*
>   *¼ teaspoon salt*
>   *¼ teaspoon allspice*
>   *½ cup mayonnaise*

Chill to blend flavors. Use as dip for
  corn chips.

Pearl of the Sea Mousse

#3   makes 1½ quarts

Put through ricer or food chopper
  6 hard-cooked eggs
Add to them
  1 cup mayonnaise
  1 teaspoon salt
  ½ teaspoon pepper
Combine and heat until smooth and liquified
  1 envelope unflavored gelatin
  2 tablespoons lemon juice
  2 tablespoons water
  1 teaspoon Worcestershire sauce
  1 teaspoon anchovy paste
  dash onion powder
Combine gelatin mixture with egg mixture. Carefully fold in
  1 (4-ounce) jar black lumpfish caviar
Decorate the bottom of a lightly greased 1½-quart ring mold with
  strips of pimiento
Spoon over the pimiento the egg and caviar mousse. Chill until
firm. Unmold and fill the center with
  black olives
Serve with
  party rye.

Peppy Almonds

#3   makes 2 cups

Melt in a flat pan
    2 teaspoons butter
Toss with
    2 cups blanched, whole almonds
Bake at 300° until lightly browned, about ½ hour. Stir often.
While still hot, sprinkle with
    seasoned salt
When cool, store in airtight container.

Pickled Cocktail Beets

#3   makes 48

Combine in a bowl
    2 cups tarragon vinegar
    4 heaping tablespoons brown sugar
    2 large onions, minced
    2 cloves garlic, mashed
    2 teaspoons dry mustard
    2 teaspoons salt
    1 teaspoon pepper
Add and marinate at least overnight
    2 (1-pound) cans whole baby beets, drained
Drain and serve.

Pickled Mushrooms

#3 makes 48

Combine and boil for 10 minutes
>2 *cups water*
>1 *cup olive oil*
>*juice of three lemons* (6 *tablespoons*)
>1 *stalk celery*
>½ *teaspoon thyme*
>½ *bay leaf*
>¾ *teaspoon ground coriander*
>8 *peppercorns*
>¾ *teaspoon salt*

Add and simmer for 5 minutes more
>48 *small whole mushroom caps*

Pour into bowl or jar, cover tightly and marinate 2 to 3 days in refrigerator. Drain and serve.

Pier 4 Cheese Spread

#3

Using mixer blend
>2 *ounces cream cheese*
>4 *tablespoons butter*

While mixture is blending add in small amounts
>2 *pounds soft Cheddar cheese spread*

Add
>1 *teaspoon prepared white horseradish*
>1 *teaspoon Worcestershire sauce*
>1 *ounce dry sherry*

Continue to blend until smooth and creamy. Serve at room temperature with
>*crackers.*

Pineapple Prosciutto

#2   makes 24

Cut into 2½-inch sticks
    1 fresh pineapple
Marinate fruit overnight in
    1 pint port wine
Drain and roll pineapple up in slices of
    1 pound prosciutto ham, very thinly sliced.

Riviera Roquefort Log

#2

Combine and beat well
    3 cups crumbled Roquefort cheese
    16 ounces cream cheese
    2 cups grated Cheddar cheese
    4 tablespoons heavy cream
Blend into cheese mixture
    ⅔ cup finely chopped walnuts
Chill 1 hour. Shape into 2 rolls each 11 inches long. Roll in
    2 cups toasted flaked coconut
Chill at least 3 hours. Cut into slices and serve on
    melba rounds or crackers.

Salmon Mousse

#2   fills 1½-quart mold

Cook together for 2 minutes but do not brown
    3 tablespoons minced onion
    1 tablespoon butter

Add and simmer for 1 minute
  2 cups chicken bouillon
  2 tablespoons gelatin, softened in
  ¼ cup dry white wine
Put the above in blender and add, buzzing for a minute or two
  2 (7¾-ounce) cans salmon
  ½ teaspoon rosemary
  ¼ teaspoon basil
Then add
  3 tablespoons dry sherry
  1 teaspoon salt
  ½ teaspoon pepper
  ¼ teaspoon nutmeg
Cover and chill until almost set. Stir occasionally. Then fold in
  ¾ cup heavy cream, whipped
Pour into a 3-cup, fish-shaped mold and chill until set. Unmold
and serve with
  crackers.

Sardine-stuffed Eggs

#1   makes 12

Remove yolks from
  6 hard-cooked eggs, halved lengthwise
Drain
  1 (3¾-ounce) can skinless and boneless sardines
Mash yolks and sardines with
  ¼ cup mayonnaise
  1 teaspoon minced onion
  1 teaspoon Worcestershire sauce
  1 tablespoon lemon juice
Refill egg whites.

Sassy Pecans

#3   makes 2 cups

Place in a shallow baking pan
> 2 *cups unsalted pecan halves*

Combine and pour over pecans
> 1 *tablespoon Worcestershire sauce*
> 1 *tablespoon salad oil*

Stir to coat all nuts.
Heat at 250° for 30 minutes. Stir occasionally. Remove from oven
and sprinkle generously with
> *garlic salt*

When cool, store in tightly covered container.

Scandinavian Herring

Chop together until very fine
> 1 *small jar herring in wine sauce, drained*
> 1 *hard-cooked egg*
> ½ *green pepper*
> 1 *tart red apple with skin*
> ½ *carrot*
> 1 *slice rye or pumpernickel soaked in vinegar*

Add more vinegar if necessary to taste.
Serve on
> *slices of party rye or pumpernickel.*

Shrimp New Orleans

#2   serves 12

    ¾ *cup Creole (hot) or brown mustard*
    ¾ *cup salad oil*
    4½ *tablespoons catsup*
    ½ *cup vinegar*
    few dashes hot pepper sauce
    3 tablespoons each finely chopped celery, green onion and
       green pepper
Add
    3 pounds cooked, cleaned medium shrimp
Cover and chill. Serve with picks.

Shrimp Pâté

#2   makes 2 cups

Combine in blender
    3 tablespoons dry sherry
    ½ *teaspoon dried tarragon*
    juice of ½ lemon (1 tablespoon)
    ½ *teaspoon mace*
    dash hot pepper sauce
    1 teaspoon Dijon mustard
    ¼ *pound butter, softened*
    salt and pepper to taste
Add 3 or 4 at a time until coarsely chopped
    1 pound cooked, shelled shrimp
Chill. Serve with
    melba toast.

Shrimps and Artichokes Vinaigrette

#2   makes 36

Chill thoroughly
> 2 (15-ounce) *cans artichoke hearts, drained and halved*
> 1½ *pounds cooked, peeled medium shrimp*

Beat together or combine in blender
> 1 *egg*
> ½ *cup vegetable oil*
> ½ *cup olive oil*
> ½ *cup wine vinegar*
> 2 *tablespoons Dijon mustard*
> 2 *tablespoons chopped chives*
> 2 *tablespoons minced scallions or onions*
> ½ *teaspoon salt*
> ½ *teaspoon sugar*
> *dash pepper*

Marinate shrimp and artichokes in dressing at least 6 hours. When ready to serve, let guests spear a shrimp and an artichoke heart on a pick.

Smoked Salmon Dip

#3   makes 3 cups

Put through meat grinder
> ½ *pound smoked salmon*

Add
> ½ *pound cream cheese*
> 1 *pint sour cream*
> 3 *green onions, chopped fine*

Let stand at least overnight in refrigerator. Serve with
> *crackers or chips.*

Smoky Egg Dip

#3

Put through blender
>6 *hard-cooked eggs*
>*enough milk to make mixture liquid enough not to stick*

While blending add
>1¼ *teaspoons liquid smoke*
>1½ *teaspoons lemon juice*
>1½ *teaspoons Worcestershire sauce*
>*dash hot pepper sauce*

Remove from blender and add
>1 *teaspoon Dijon mustard*
>1 *tablespoon soft butter*
>¾ *teaspoon salt*
>⅛ *teaspoon freshly ground black pepper*
>6 *tablespoons mayonnaise*
>½ *teaspoon minced onion*

Mix until smooth. Refrigerate. To serve, surround with
>*lightly seasoned crackers.*

Snappy Cheese Apple

*#3

Mix together and form into shape of an apple
>¾ *pound sharp Cheddar cheese, grated*
>¼ *pound Swiss cheese, grated*
>1 *(3-ounce) package cream cheese*
>1 *tablespoon prepared mustard*
>1 *teaspoon Worcestershire sauce*

Sprinkle generously with
>*chili powder*

Make stem with
>*cinnamon stick*

Refrigerate or freeze. To serve, bring to room temperature. Slice
and serve with
    crackers.

Tivoli Clam Dip

#3

Mash
    ¼ pound blue cheese
Blend with
    ½ pint sour cream
and stir until smooth and creamy. Stir in
    2 (8-ounce) cans minced clams, drained
    2 teaspoons Worcestershire sauce
Chill until serving time. Then garnish with
    capers
Serve with vegetable dippers such as
    celery, cucumber slices, endive spears, cauliflowerets.

Toasted Almond Dip

#2   makes about 4 cups

Combine and mix well
    2 packages dry onion soup mix
    2 pints sour cream
    ½ cup chopped toasted almonds
    1 teaspoon curry powder
    generous dash garlic powder
Chill. Serve with
    chips or crackers.

Zippy Avocado

#2

Peel and stone
>2 *large avocados*

Hard cook and shell
>6 *eggs*

Peel and chop
>1 *large onion*

Combine avocado, eggs and onion and chop them very fine until smooth and well blended. Add
>½ *teaspoon chili powder*
>¼ *cup chopped parsley*
>2 *tablespoons vinegar*
>2 *tablespoons salt*

Mix thoroughly and refrigerate at least 24 hours to blend flavors. Serve as a dip with
>*corn chips.*

Meat Main Dishes

Beef in Aspic

#2   serves 10

Not only is this recipe easy, but it is just perfect for your weight-watching guests.

Arrange

    20 thin slices medium-rare roast beef or fillet of beef (can be leftover!)

on two or more platters or in shallow casseroles.

Combine a few tablespoons from

    1 (10½-ounce) can beef consommé (the kind that jells when chilled)

with

    1 teaspoon unflavored gelatin

Dissolve and return to remaining consommé. Heat until completely dissolved. Pour a thin layer of consommé over beef and allow to set. Decorate beef with

    2 (8-ounce) jars marinated mushrooms
    2 (12½-ounce) jars Belgian baby carrots
    4 hard-cooked eggs, sliced
    pimiento
    parsley

Pour over more consommé. When jellied, paint any remaining uncoated food with a little of consommé and chill again. Cut into pieces to serve.

NOTE: If you are roasting meat you know will be used in this recipe, you can brush it with a mixture of soy sauce, dry sherry, thyme and garlic. Brush it every 20 minutes or so.

Beef 'n' Beer

* # 2   serves 6

Brown a little at a time in a large Dutch oven
   3 pounds chuck steak, cut into 1-inch cubes
   3 onions, chopped
   1½ cloves garlic, crushed
in
   ¾ cup butter or margarine
Add
   ½ cup flour
Mix flour with other ingredients to coat them well. Combine and
pour over meat
   1½ cups beef consommé
   1½ cups beer
Season with
   3 tablespoons brown sugar
   1½ tablespoons minced parsley
   2 bay leaves
   1½ teaspoons thyme
   salt and pepper to taste
Bake in 300° oven until meat is tender, about 3 hours. Cool. Reheat on top of stove when ready to serve.

Beef with Oyster Sauce

* # 1   serves 8

Combine and use as marinade
   ½ cup soy sauce
   2 tablespoons sherry
   ½ teaspoon powdered ginger
   1 tablespoon seasoned salt
Marinate in this for at least 2 hours
   4 pounds flank steak, sliced thin across the grain

Mix together
>   2 *teaspoons sugar*
>   2 *tablespoons cornstarch*
>   4 *tablespoons water*
>   4 *tablespoons oyster sauce (oriental bottled sauce available at most specialty food stores)*

In a large skillet heat
>   4 *tablespoons peanut oil*

Stir in the steak and
>   4 *green onions, sliced*

Add and stir-fry for 3 to 4 minutes
>   2 *(4-ounce) cans button mushrooms, drained*
>   2 *packages frozen pea pods*

Add sauce and stir thoroughly. Cover and simmer for 5 minutes. Reheat to serve.

Cannelloni

* # 2   serves 8 people 3 crepes each

The most elegant cannelloni you ever saw or ate. Make the crepes one day. Make the sauce another. Make the filling; fill the crepes; sauce them and refrigerate or freeze.

Crepes

* # 1   makes 24

In a small bowl stir with wire whisk until quite smooth
>   8 *heaping tablespoons flour*
>   2 *eggs*
>   2 *egg yolks*
>   6 *tablespoons milk*
>   2 *tablespoons vegetable oil*

Use enough from
> 2 cups milk to make batter of thin consistency

Refrigerate for 3 to 4 hours. (It may be kept in refrigerator up to a week.) Remove and add enough of remaining milk to reduce again to thin consistency, between light and heavy cream. Heat 6- or 7-inch frying pan (crepe); when very hot wipe out with piece of slightly buttered wax paper. Return to lowered heat. Cover bottom of pan with very thin layer of batter. (Pour off excess.) Cook until golden on one side; turn and cook until golden on other side. Stack them as they cook. Using the same piece of wax paper, rebuttering it occasionally, rub the bottom of the pan between each crepe.

Freeze crepes, stacked, and fill them after defrosting, or use them for any recipes calling for crepes and freeze them filled.

Filling

Steam and extract as much moisture as possible from
> 1 package frozen spinach

Add to
> 1 cup ricotta cheese

Melt in large pan
> 4 tablespoons butter

Blend in
> ¼ cup flour

Slowly add
> ½ cup milk

Heat and stir until thickened.
Regrind
> ½ pound ground chuck

with
> 3 ounces mushrooms

directly into sauce; mix thoroughly and continue cooking over medium heat until paste begins to bubble and beef is browning. Cook another 2 to 3 minutes, then add
> ¼ cup grated Parmesan cheese
> few dashes nutmeg
> salt and pepper

Remove from heat and cool. Stir in ricotta and spinach. Taste for seasoning; refrigerate if not using right away.

Tomato Sauce

* # 1

Heat
> ¼ *cup olive oil*
> *4 tablespoons butter*

In it sauté until soft
> *1 onion, minced*
> *1 clove garlic, minced*
> *1 carrot, minced*
> *1 stalk celery, minced*
> *good pinch basil*

Add
> *4 pounds peeled and coarsely chopped tomatoes or 3 (1-
> pound, 12-ounce) cans Italian plum tomatoes*
> *sprinkling of sugar*
> *salt and freshly ground black pepper*

Bring to boil. Reduce heat and simmer slowly, covered, for 2 to
3 hours. Stir occasionally.

THE FINAL ASSEMBLY
> *6 ounces coarsely ground mozzarella*
> *24 crepes*
> *Filling*
> *Tomato Sauce*

Butter square baking dish that you can take to the table and
spoon a layer of tomato sauce on the bottom. Fill each crepe
with dessertspoonful of filling. Spread it over crepe and roll up.
Arrange crepes side by side. Cover with tomato sauce and sprinkle
with coarsely ground mozzarella cheese. Bake at 400° for 15 to 25
minutes, to heat thoroughly.

Cassoulet

1   serves 8

Combine and soak overnight
> *5 cups great northern beans*

Drain, discarding any that are floating. Put in large kettle with
> ½ *pound fresh pork rind, which has been blanched in boiling*
> *water*
> ½ *pound salt pork*

In a cheesecloth bag make a bouquet garni of
> 1 *onion stuck with a clove*
> 1 *bunch parsley*
> 1 *carrot*
> 3 *sprigs celery leaves*
> 2 *cloves garlic*
> 1 *bay leaf*
> ½ *teaspoon thyme*

Add to kettle, cover with boiling water and return to boil. Reduce
heat, cover and simmer for 1 hour. Add
> ½ *pound garlic sausage*

Simmer 1½ hours or until beans are just tender.
While beans are cooking melt in skillet
> ¼ *cup lard*

In it brown
> 2 *pounds boned breast of lamb, cut in chunks*
> ½ *pound pork sausage links*
> ½ *pound garlic frankfurters or knackwurst*

Remove the meat and brown
> 2 *onions, finely chopped*
> 1 *clove garlic, minced*

Put browned meat, onions and garlic in a casserole, add
> *salt and pepper*

and moisten with
> ¼ *cup beef consommé*

Cover casserole and cook meat at 325° for 1¾ hours or until lamb
is tender. Add more simmering liquid (consommé) when necessary. Drain cooked beans and reserve liquid. Discard pork rind
and salt pork. Slice garlic sausage and reserve. Combine with beans
> ½ *cup white wine*
> ½ *cup tomato purée*

The beans must be moist but not floating. Add as much of reserved bean liquid as necessary. Stir in
> 1 *tablespoon minced parsley*

Adjust seasonings.
In large casserole arrange layers of beans and layers of combined meats.
Each layer must be seasoned with
   pepper
sprinkled lightly with
   sage (using 2 teaspoons in all)
and dampened with reserve bean liquid to keep cassoulet moist.
End with bean layer and top with reserved garlic sausage. Cover casserole and bake at 300° for 1 hour. Cool. Refrigerate overnight.
To serve, heat at 300° for 1½ hours.

Chili Cheese Jubilee

* #1   serves 6 to 8

Brown in a skillet until crumbly
   1 pound ground chuck
in
   2 tablespoons shortening
Melt in another skillet
   2 tablespoons butter
In it sauté until tender
   1 medium onion, chopped
Add to onion
   1 (8-ounce) can tomato sauce
   1 (1¼-ounce) package chili seasoning mix
   ½ cup water
Simmer for 5 minutes. Beat slightly and add
   2 eggs
   1 cup light cream
On bottom of 2-quart casserole, place
   ½ (11-ounce) package corn chips
Top with half of browned beef and a layer of
   Monterey Jack cheese (if not available use Cheddar cheese)
      (use 8 ounces total)

Cover with half of sauce. Repeat layers.
Top with
>   *1 cup sour cream*
Sprinkle with
>   *½ cup grated Cheddar cheese*
Refrigerate or freeze. When ready to serve, defrost and bake at
325° for 25 to 30 minutes.

Colton Manor Moussaka

*# 3   serves 12

In
>   *2 tablespoons olive oil*
sauté
>   *3 large onions, chopped*
>   *1 green pepper, chopped*
>   *2 cloves garlic, minced*
After 10 minutes add
>   *6 small zucchini, finely chopped*
>   *1 unpeeled eggplant, finely chopped*
When ingredients are softened add
>   *1 (1-pound, 12-ounce) can tomatoes, drained*
>   *2 teaspoons Worcestershire sauce*
>   *few dashes hot pepper sauce*
>   *nutmeg to taste*
>   *salt and pepper to taste*
Cook these ingredients down until they can't be distinguished
from each other. Before adding to casserole, drain off all excess
liquid. Meanwhile, brown
>   *2 pounds ground chuck*
Add
>   *1 large onion, finely chopped*
>   *1 clove garlic, minced*
and cook for 15 minutes.

Add

> 1 (8-ounce) can tomato sauce
> salt to taste
> nutmeg to taste

Simmer for 15 minutes.
Make a thick cream sauce as follows: Melt

> 4 tablespoons butter

Stir in

> 4 tablespoons flour

Off the heat add

> 2 cups milk

Return to low heat and cook, stirring until very thick. Season with

> 1 teaspoon Worcestershire sauce
> hot pepper sauce to taste
> salt to taste

In one or two casseroles layer the mixtures. Place in the bottom the meat mixture.
Top with

> ¾ to 1 cup grated Parmesan cheese

Then add eggplant mixture. Top with

> ¾ to 1 cup grated Parmesan cheese

Top with cream sauce. Sprinkle on

> ¾ to 1 cup grated Parmesan cheese

Freeze or refrigerate. To serve, return to room temperature and bake at 350° for about 1 hour, until top is brown and mixture is bubbly.

Herbed Veal

* # 2   serves 6

Shake in a paper bag

> 4 pounds cubed boneless veal
> ½ cup flour
> ½ teaspoon seasoned salt
> ¼ teaspoon seasoned pepper

Saving the flour, remove the veal pieces and brown them in a skillet with

>   ½ *cup butter*

Remove the veal from the skillet and in the same butter brown

>   ½ *cup finely chopped onions*
>   ½ *pound fresh mushrooms, sliced*

When onions are wilted, stir in remaining flour and

>   ¼ *teaspoon rosemary*
>   1 *tablespoon chopped fresh parsley*
>   ⅔ *cup dry white wine*
>   2 *tablespoons lemon juice*
>   1 *teaspoon sugar*
>   2 *cups canned tomatoes*

Bring just to a boil and add veal; cover and simmer for 45 minutes. When ready to serve, reheat.

Meat Balls Piemonte

* # 2   serves 8

Combine and mix well

>   3 *pounds ground chuck*
>   ¾ *clove garlic, crushed*
>   1½ *medium onions, finely chopped*
>   ½ *teaspoon each savory, orégano and paprika*
>   1 *tablespoon salt*
>   1½ *cups seasoned bread crumbs*
>   1½ *tablespoons prepared mustard*
>   *few dashes hot pepper sauce*
>   1 *tablespoon Worcestershire sauce*

Form into 3 to 4 dozen 1½- to 2-inch balls. Dust with

>   *flour*

Cook until crisp and brown

>   6 *strips bacon, cut in small pieces*

Remove from pan. Sauté meat balls in bacon drippings until lightly browned. Add

1½ *cups strong coffee*
¾ *cup Burgundy wine*
1½ *teaspoons salt*
1½ *teaspoons sugar*
Simmer 15 minutes. Return bacon to pan. Stir in
2¼ *tablespoons flour*
mixed smooth with
½ *cup cold water*
Refrigerate or freeze. To serve, return to room temperature and heat until hot throughout. Garnish with dollops from
1½ *cups sour cream*
If the meat balls are made smaller, they are perfect for hors d'oeuvres.

Neapolitan Veal

#1   serves 8

Between two pieces of wax paper pound thin
8 *slices veal scallops, cut less than ¼ inch thick*
Dust with
salt
pepper
flour
Heat in large skillet or skillets
3 *tablespoons butter*
Sauté 2 scallops at a time so they will brown. Remove and keep warm. Repeat until all are brown. Then return all to pan(s). In another pan heat
6 *tablespoons brandy*
Ignite and pour over veal. Remove veal from pan and stir juices well. Add
1½ *tablespoons butter*
Remove from heat and stir in
1½ *teaspoons meat glaze*
1½ *teaspoons tomato paste*
1 *tablespoon arrowroot*

Then add
>   2 *cups chicken stock*
>   ½ *cup dry white wine*
>   3 *tablespoons sherry*
>   1½ *teaspoons currant jelly*

Return to heat and bring to boil. Reduce heat; add veal and simmer gently with pan covered for 10 minutes. Meanwhile halve lengthwise and slice ¼ inch thick
>   3 *zucchini*

Place in pan with cold water to cover and bring to boil. Drain and return zucchini to pan with
>   2 *tablespoons butter*
>   ¾ *teaspoon salt*
>   *freshly ground black pepper*

Cover with buttered wax paper and tight-fitting lid; cook for 5 minutes. In frying pan heat
>   6 *tablespoons butter*

Add
>   8 *skinned and thickly sliced tomatoes*
>   1 *tablespoon chopped garlic*
>   *freshly ground black pepper*

Cook briskly for 2 minutes. Mix zucchini and tomatoes gently but well. Arrange the vegetables on the bottom of oval ovenproof serving dish. Place veal slices on top, overlapping one another. On top of veal slices place
>   8 *slices imported Swiss cheese*

Pour sauce over. Sprinkle with
>   *freshly grated Parmesan cheese*
>   *melted butter*

Refrigerate if desired. To serve, bring to room temperature and heat at 350° for about 20 minutes, until heated through. Run under broiler until cheese is browned.

Pasta Florentine

* # 2   serves 8 to 10

In
> 2 tablespoons shortening

brown until crumbly
> 1½ pounds ground chuck

Add and simmer 20 minutes
> 2 cloves garlic, crushed
> 1 medium onion, chopped
> 2 packages spaghetti sauce mix
> 1½ teaspoons seasoned salt
> ½ teaspoon seasoned pepper
> 1 (6-ounce) can tomato paste
> ¾ cup water
> 1 (1-pound, 12-ounce) can tomatoes

Add and simmer 5 minutes more
> ¼ cup dry sherry

Spoon off excess fat.

Cook according to package directions until barely tender, then drain and set aside
> 1 (8-ounce) package bow tie macaroni

Cook according to package directions but without salt
> 1 (10-ounce) package frozen chopped spinach

Drain spinach well, then cool. Combine
> 2 eggs, beaten
> ¼ cup fine dry bread crumbs
> ½ cup grated Parmesan cheese
> ½ teaspoon seasoned salt
> 1 (4-ounce) can mushroom stems and pieces, drained and
>   chopped
> 1 (2¼-ounce) can sliced ripe olives, drained
> spinach

Place half macaroni on bottom of buttered 3-quart casserole. Cover with half spinach mixture, then half the meat mixture. Repeat layers. Top with
> ¼ cup grated Parmesan cheese

Refrigerate or freeze. When ready to serve, bring to room temperature and bake at 350° for 30 to 40 minutes.

Sour Cream Noodle Bake

* # 2   serves 6

A *simple, informal buffet main dish.*
Cook according to package directions, then rinse and drain
    1 (8-ounce) package medium egg noodles
Melt in skillet
    2 tablespoons butter or margarine
Add, stir, and cook until it loses its pink color
    1 pound ground chuck
Add
    1 (8-ounce) can tomato sauce
    1 teaspoon salt
    ¼ teaspoon garlic salt
    ⅛ teaspoon pepper
Cover and simmer 5 minutes.
Fold together
    noodles
    1 cup cottage cheese
    1 cup sour cream
    ½ cup green onions, chopped
Spoon half the mixture into bottom of 2½-quart casserole. Cover with half of meat mixture. Repeat layers once again. Sprinkle with
    ¾ cup coarsely shredded Cheddar cheese
Refrigerate or freeze. When ready to serve, return to room temperature and bake at 350° for 30 to 35 minutes or until mixture is heated through and cheese is melted.

South Sea Beef

Sweet and sour beef with an added touch.
Brown
>   4 *pounds 1-inch beef cubes (sirloin or rib)*

in
>   ½ *cup hot salad oil*

Drain, reserving syrup,
>   2 *(20-ounce) cans pineapple chunks*

Add syrup to skillet with
>   2 *tablespoons plus 2 teaspoons soy sauce*
>   2 *tablespoons vinegar*

Bring to boil; reduce heat and simmer 15 minutes. Add pineapple chunks and
>   2 *cups diced celery*
>   2 *cucumbers, thinly sliced*
>   2 *tomatoes, peeled and cut in wedges*
>   2 *green peppers, cut in 1-inch squares*
>   2 *medium onions, thinly sliced*

Cook 5 more minutes. Combine and stir until smooth
>   4 *teaspoons cornstarch*
>   4 *tablespoons water*

Gradually add to beef mixture and cook, stirring constantly, until mixture thickens and comes to a boil. You may prepare this dish a day in advance up to the point where cornstarch is added. Finish cooking by returning mixture to room temperature and continuing with directions.
To serve, spoon
>   6 *cups hot cooked rice (2 cups when raw)*

around edge of platter; turn hot beef mixture into center.

Spicy Buffet Beef

* # 3   serves 8

In heavy pan or Dutch oven brown
    4-pound brisket of beef
Add
    1 large onion, diced
    salt to taste
Turn heat low enough so meat just simmers when covered. Cook
until tender, about 2½ to 3 hours.
Combine and simmer for an hour
    1 (14-ounce) bottle catsup
    1 large onion, diced
    1 heaping tablespoon brown sugar
    1⅓ tablespoons Worcestershire sauce
    1⅔ cups water
    1 tablespoon dry mustard
    1 tablespoon vinegar
    ½ teaspoon chili powder
    ⅓ teaspoon paprika
    1 clove garlic, minced
When beef is tender, remove from juices. Slice the beef in small
pieces and pour the sauce over. Refrigerate or freeze. To serve,
reheat and serve hot from chafing dish with small, soft rolls.

Sweet and Sour Beef

* # 2   serves 8

Brown
    4 pounds chuck cut in 1-inch cubes
in own fat after seasoning with
    salt and pepper

Add
>   1 *cup water*
>   1 *cup catsup*
>   ½ *cup brown sugar*
>   ½ *cup wine vinegar*
>   2 *tablespoons Worcestershire sauce*
>   2 *teaspoons salt*
>   ⅔ *cup raisins*
>   2 *large onions, chopped*

Cover and simmer for 30 minutes. Add
>   6 *carrots, cut in ¼-inch rounds*

Cook 30 to 45 minutes longer, until tender.

Tenderloin Stuffed with Ham

* #1   serves 8

This is for a small, very elegant buffet.
Sauté until limp
>   3 *large onions, thinly sliced*

in
>   6 *tablespoons olive oil*
>   4 *tablespoons butter*

Then add
>   2 *cloves garlic, minced*
>   1 *(4½-ounce) can chopped ripe olives*
>   ½ *cup chopped cooked country ham*
>   1 *teaspoon freshly ground black pepper*
>   1 *teaspoon thyme*
>   *salt to taste, if necessary*

Cook until all of mixture is very well blended. Stir in
>   2 *egg yolks, beaten*
>   2 *tablespoons chopped parsley*

Cook a few minutes and stir until blended.
Cut into 8 to 10 thick slices—not quite through to bottom—
>   1 *whole fillet of beef*

Spoon the stuffing between the slices. At the thin tail end, fold over the tail on some stuffing. Then skewer the stuffing and fillet with a skewer running from one end through to the other end. Freeze or refrigerate. When ready to serve, return to room temperature and roast at 300° for 50 minutes on rack. Brush once with oil. Let rest 10 minutes, salt lightly and slice through. Serve on platter decorated with watercress.

Tomato-glazed Beef

serves 8

Let sit at room temperature for 1 hour before roasting
  5-pound sirloin tip roast
Roast at 375° for 10 minutes. Reduce heat to 325° and roast, allowing 20 minutes per pound. When figuring roasting time, allow 15 minutes for roast to stand before carving. Baste meat as it roasts every 20 minutes with the following sauce:

Tomato Glaze:
Combine and simmer for 5 minutes
  1 (8-ounce) can tomato sauce
  ½ cup dry white wine
  ½ cup salad oil
  1 tablespoon sugar
  ½ teaspoon chili powder
  1 teaspoon salt
  ½ teaspoon basil
  ½ cup finely chopped onion
Serve warm, sliced medium thick.

Veal Flamenco

* # 2   serves 8

Cut into cubes
   4 pounds boneless veal
Sauté meat in mixture of
   ¼ cup butter
   ¼ cup olive oil
until well browned. Transfer meat to casserole. Add
   16 small white onions, peeled
   2 teaspoons sugar
Cook over low heat until onions are lightly browned. Add
   2 canned pimientos, chopped
   4 carrots, cubed
Sauté briefly. Then add
   1 (8-ounce) can tomato sauce
   2 cups dry white wine
   1 tablespoon salt
Simmer 5 minutes; add sauce and vegetables to meat in casserole.
Freeze, if desired, or refrigerate. To serve, return to room temperature and bake at 350° for about 3 hours or cook on top of
the stove at lowest possible heat until meat is tender. Sprinkle
with
   2 tablespoons minced parsley
and serve.

Veal Marengo

* # 2   serves 10

Roll
   5 pounds boneless veal, cut in 1½-inch cubes
in
   5 tablespoons flour

Heat
    ½ cup vegetable oil
in skillet. Add meat and cook over moderate heat about 5 minutes,
stirring frequently. Add
    4 tablespoons finely chopped onion
    4 large cloves garlic, crushed or finely chopped
Cook 5 minutes.
Rub through sieve
    2 (1-pound, 3-ounce) cans tomatoes
and add to meat. Add
    1 cup chicken broth
    3 cups dry white wine
    2 teaspoons salt
    ½ teaspoon pepper
    2 teaspoons orégano
Cover and simmer gently 1 hour, stirring once in a while. Meanwhile melt in another skillet
    4 tablespoons butter
Add
    24 mushroom caps
and cook over moderate heat until lightly browned. Peel
    12 medium-sized whole white onions
Add mushrooms and onions to meat. Refrigerate or freeze. To
serve, return to room temperature and cook for ½ hour, or until
meat and onions are tender.
Just before serving, stir in
    2 cups heavy cream
and heat but do not boil.

Veal Milanese

* # 1   serves 8

Sauté until soft
    2 medium onions, chopped

in

    4 tablespoons olive oil

Add

    2 (6-ounce) cans tomato paste
    2 (10-ounce) cans beef consommé
    2 soup cans water
    1½ teaspoons crumbled thyme
    ½ teaspoon rosemary
    1 tablespoon salt
    ½ teaspoon pepper
    2 teaspoons sugar

Cover and simmer 1½ hours, stirring occasionally. In a large frying pan, add

    4 tablespoons olive oil
    4 tablespoons butter

Brown

    3½ pounds boneless veal, cut in bite-sized chunks

Remove from pan. In fat in same pan sauté

    1 pound mushrooms, sliced

Add to tomato sauce

    3 cups white wine
    veal
    mushrooms
    1 cup sliced, pitted ripe olives

Cover. Simmer 1 hour. Refrigerate or freeze. To serve, defrost, re-heat and add

    2 (9-ounce) packages frozen artichoke hearts, cooked and
        drained

Serve on

    noodles.

Poultry Main Dishes

Chicken Livers Gourmet

serves 12

In skillet melt
>   ¼ cup butter

Sauté in it until they begin to brown
>   2 medium onions, finely chopped

Stir in and sauté for 3 to 4 minutes
>   4 pounds mushrooms, sliced, or 4 (8-ounce) cans sliced mushrooms, drained

Add
>   4 pounds chicken livers

and sauté quickly until they have lost all their pinkness. Combine
>   3 tablespoons soy sauce
>   ⅓ cup chili sauce
>   3 cups sour cream
>   3 cups dry red wine

Stir into chicken livers and season to taste with
>   salt and freshly ground black pepper

Refrigerate if desired. To serve, bring to room temperature and heat through gently. Do not allow to boil or the sour cream will curdle.

Chicken Lo Mein

*# 1   serves 8

Boil, drain and set aside
> 1 *pound fine shrimp noodles (available where Chinese foods*
> *are sold, or use regular fine noodles)*

Soak for 15 minutes and set aside
> 8 *dried mushrooms*

in
> ⅔ *cup hot water (reserve water)*

Wash, dry and chop
> 1 *pound fresh spinach*
> 2 *bunches green onions*

Heat in a deep pot over high flame
> 4 *tablespoons oil*

Add spinach and green onions and toss for 3 minutes. Add
> *mushrooms*
> 4 *cups cubed cooked chicken*
> 2 *(1-pound) cans Chinese vegetables, drained*
> 2 *teaspoons sugar*
> 2 *cups chicken stock*

Cover and simmer for 10 minutes.
Combine
> 3 *tablespoons cornstarch*
> 4 *tablespoons soy sauce*
> *reserved mushroom water*

Add to chicken mixture and stir until smooth and thick. Add salt
and pepper to taste. Add cooked noodles and stir gently until
heated through. Refrigerate or freeze. When ready to serve, reheat
in top of double boiler.

Chicken Tahitian

#1   serves 6

Marinate
>   *6 chicken breasts, boned and halved*

in
>   *2 tablespoons lemon juice*
>   *1 teaspoon ground ginger*

Broil breasts for 10 minutes on each side, dotting them with
>   *6 tablespoons butter*

Sprinkle them with
>   *1 teaspoon salt*
>   *¼ teaspoon pepper*

Stir together over low heat
>   *6 tablespoons pan drippings*
>   *6 tablespoons flour*

Remove from heat and stir in
>   *2 cups milk*

Return to heat and cook until very thick, then add
>   *1 cup unsweetened pineapple juice*
>   *½ teaspoon ground ginger*

In bottom of casserole place chicken breasts and
>   *4 cups cooked rice*

Cover all with sauce to which you add
>   *½ cup chopped macadamia nuts*

When ready to serve, bake uncovered at 350° for 20 to 30 minutes.

Chutney Chicken Salad

#1   serves 8

In large bowl combine
> 1 *cup mayonnaise*
> ¼ *cup chopped chutney*
> 1 *teaspoon curry powder*
> 2 *teaspoons grated lime peel*
> ¼ *cup fresh lime juice*
> ½ *teaspoon salt*

Blend well and stir in
> 4 *cups diced, cooked white meat chicken*
> 2 (13¼-*ounce*) *cans pineapple chunks, drained*
> 2 *cups diagonally sliced celery*
> 1 *cup sliced green onions*
> ½ *cup toasted whole blanched almonds*

Serve on crisp salad greens.

Green Noodles Chicken

* #1   serves 10

Simmer with just enough water to cover
> 1 (5-*pound*) *hen or 2 broilers, cut in pieces*

with
> 1 *onion*
> 1 *carrot*
> *salt to taste*

Let stock cool and fat harden for use in sauce. Cool chicken in stock. Remove fat. Then remove meat from skin and bones. Cut in large pieces. Strain stock and reserve.

Cook according to package directions
> 8 *ounces green* (or *spinach*) *noodles*

Drain and rinse in cold water; drain well. Butter a 9 x 13-inch glass dish.

Melt

    ½ cup butter or ½ cup fat from chicken

Blend in

    ⅔ cup flour

Cook, stirring, a few minutes. Gradually add

    3 cups reserved chicken stock

    1 (8-ounce) can mushrooms and liquid

    ¾ teaspoon garlic powder

    1 teaspoon salt

Mix until smooth. Add

    3 tablespoons dry white wine

    5 cups grated Parmesan cheese

Cook until thickened.

Layer

    noodles

    chicken

    sauce

in baking dish, using two layers of each. Refrigerate or freeze. When ready to serve, return to room temperature, then bake at 350° for 30 to 45 minutes. While baking sauté

    3 to 4 cups bread, torn into ¾-inch pieces

in

    4 tablespoons butter

About 5 minutes before chicken is done, spread crumbs and

    4 ounces slivered almonds

on top of casserole and return to oven to brown quickly.

Rolled Chicken Breasts

#1   serves 8

Pound as thin as possible, without tearing

    8 whole chicken breasts, split in half and boned

On each half breast place
> 1 *teaspoon finely chopped green onion*
> 1 *teaspoon finely chopped parsley*
> 1 *teaspoon butter*

Roll up breasts and dip them in
> 1 *cup flour*

then in
> 2 *eggs beaten*

then in
> 1 *cup cornflake crumbs*

Let stand at least 1 hour or as long as overnight. Place in a shallow pan and top with
> ½ *cup butter*
> ½ *cup dry sherry*

Cover pan with foil and bake at 350° for 1 hour, then uncover and continue baking for another 30 minutes. Baste occasionally.

Rosemary Chicken-Tangerine Rice

#1   serves 8

Rosemary Wine Seasoning:
Crush
> 2½ *tablespoons dried rosemary*

into
> ⅔ *cup dry vermouth*
> 3 *tablespoons water*

Allow to stand in warm place for 1 hour.

Tangerine Butter:
Combine
> 2 *tablespoons melted butter*
> 6 *tablespoons frozen tangerine juice concentrate, undiluted*
> 1 *tablespoon dry vermouth*
> 1 *teaspoon salt*
> ¼ *teaspoon pepper*

Wash and pat dry
>3 (3½-pound) *frying chickens, cut in pieces*

Dip them in
>½ *cup orange juice*

Dust them lightly with
>*seasoned flour (¾ cup flour, 1½ teaspoons salt, ½ teaspoon ginger, ¼ teaspoon pepper)*

Brown chicken in large skillet for 20 minutes in
>6 *tablespoons butter*
>6 *tablespoons vegetable oil*

Add Rosemary Wine Seasoning, cover loosely and simmer 15 to 20 minutes, until liquid is evaporated, chicken tender but not quite done.

Cook as directed on package
>1½ *cups raw rice*

Toss rice together with
>*Tangerine Butter*
>6 *green onions, sliced, white part only*
>1 (1-pound) *package frozen peas, thawed and separated*
>1 (4-ounce) *can pimientos, sliced*

Spread rice mixture on bottom of two 9 x 13-inch baking dishes. Arrange chicken in single layer over rice. When ready to serve, cover and bake at 375° for 20 minutes. Remove cover and bake 10 minutes more until heated through. Pile chicken in center. Decorate with
>2 *avocados, sliced in wedges*
>1 (29-ounce) *can whole apricots, drained.*

Swedish Chicken Salad

#1   serves 8

Roast, then cool, skin, bone and cut into strips
>2 (3½-pound) *chickens*

Cook according to package directions, then chill
>2 *cups raw rice*

Core and slice
> 2 *red apples*
> 2 *green apples*

Slice, then dredge with lemon juice
> 2 *bananas*

Whip
> ½ *pint heavy cream*

Fold cream into
> 1 *cup mayonnaise*
> *juice and grated rind of ½ lemon*
> 1 *teaspoon curry powder*

Fold in chicken and fruit. Add more lemon juice to taste. Pile on bed of rice to serve.

Sea Food Main Dishes

Chesapeake Crab

 # 1 serves 8

Every good Marylander has some version of this delicious dish.
Mix together

    1 cup mayonnaise
    2 tablespoons Worcestershire sauce
    ¼ cup finely chopped green pepper
    ¼ cup finely chopped onion
    1½ whole canned pimientos, chopped
    1 teaspoon dry mustard
    1 teaspoon salt
    3 tablespoons dry sherry

Stir in

    2 eggs

Pick over and remove any shell from

    2 pounds lump or backfin crabmeat

Gently fold crab into sauce mixture. Lumps should stay lumps—
they should not break up into shreds. Turn into large casserole
and sprinkle lightly with

    bread crumbs

Dot with

    butter

Sprinkle with

    paprika

Refrigerate. To serve, return to room temperature, then bake at
350° for 30 to 40 minutes, until thoroughly heated and top is
lightly browned.

Exotic Shrimp Salad

#1   serves 12

Toss together
>   *4 pounds cooked, cleaned shrimp*
>   *2 cups sliced water chestnuts*
>   *½ cup minced green onions*
>   *½ cup diced celery*
>   *1½ cups mayonnaise*
>   *4 teaspoons curry powder*
>   *4 tablespoons soy sauce*

Arrange salad in
>   *lettuce cups*

Garnish with
>   *1 cup toasted slivered almonds.*

Fisherman's Find

#1   serves 8

Combine
>   *1 cup cooked lobster meat*
>   *1 cup cooked crabmeat*
>   *½ pound cooked shrimp*
>   *1 cup cooked white fish (flounder, sole)*
>   *3 tomatoes, sliced*
>   *⅓ cup sliced ripe olives*
>   *1 small head iceberg lettuce, in bite-sized pieces*
>   *½ head celery cabbage, in bite-sized pieces*
>   *1 bunch watercress, cut up*
>   *1 bunch celery tops, cut up*
>   *3 green onions, cut up*

When ready to serve, toss with dressing made by combining
> ¼ *cup tarragon vinegar*
> ⅔ *cup salad oil*
> 3 *tablespoons grated onion*
> 1 *bay leaf, crumbled*
> ¼ *teaspoon chili powder*
> ⅛ *teaspoon cayenne*
> ½ *teaspoon salt*
> ¼ *teaspoon pepper*
> 2 *tablespoons sugar.*

Paella Salad

#1   serves 12

In a large skillet, heat
> 6 *tablespoons salad oil*

Add and cook until golden
> ¾ *cup finely chopped onion*

Dissolve
> 3 *chicken bouillon cubes*

in
> 2 *cups boiling water*

Add bouillon to skillet along with
> ¼ *teaspoon hot pepper sauce*
> ¼ *teaspoon curry powder*
> 4 *strands saffron*

Bring to a full boil, then stir in
> 2 *cups instant rice*

Cover. Remove from heat and let stand 5 minutes. Fluff with a fork to mix seasonings. Chill thoroughly. At least 1 hour before serving, combine

5 *pounds mixed cooked sea food* (*shrimp, lobster, tuna, mussels*)
1½ *green peppers, diced*
1 (*4-ounce*) *can pimiento, diced*
¾ *pound mushrooms, sliced*
chilled rice
¾ *cup Italian dressing*
Arrange in salad bowl and serve with additional dressing.

Scallop Casserole

#1   serves 6

Arrange on bottom of 2-quart casserole
  2 *pounds scallops* (*if large, cut in quarters*)
Combine and pour over the scallops
  1 *egg yolk, beaten*
  ½ *cup light cream*
  ¼ *cup white wine*
  2 *teaspoons lemon juice*
  1 *tablespoon minced onion*
  ⅛ *teaspoon white pepper*
  ⅛ *teaspoon ground ginger*
  1½ *teaspoons salt*
Combine and use as topping
  1 *cup soft bread crumbs*
  2 *tablespoons melted butter*
  2 *tablespoons grated Parmesan cheese*
When ready to serve, bake at 350° for 30 minutes; raise heat to 450° for 5 minutes to brown crumbs on top.

Seafood Santa Barbara

#1 serves 6

Blend and chill
>   ¾ *cup mayonnaise*
>   ¾ *cup chili sauce*
>   1½ *tablespoons Worcestershire sauce*
>   1½ *tablespoons prepared white horseradish*
>   1½ *tablespoons lemon juice*
>   *dash cayenne pepper*

Toss with half the above dressing
>   ¾ *pound cooked shrimp, coarsely chopped*
>   ¾ *cup fresh crabmeat*
>   1½ *cups fresh diced lobster*

Use sea food to fill
>   6 *artichokes, cooked and chilled, leaves spread and centers*
>   *removed.*

Serve with remaining dressing and
>   *lemon wedges*

For a large crowd, where you do not wish to use individual artichokes, you may use artichoke hearts for garnish.

Tarragon Crab

#1 serves 4

Marinate for an hour
>   1½ *pounds backfin crabmeat, picked over to remove any shell*

in
>   ½ *cup tarragon vinegar*

Pour off vinegar. Combine
>   ¾ *cup mayonnaise*

with

3 *tablespoons chopped sour pickle*
3 *tablespoons chopped parsley*
3 *tablespoons chopped chives*
1½ *teaspoons onion juice*

Combine crab and mayonnaise mixture.
This is nice if served in scallop shells. Top each portion with
   well-drained capers.

Vitello Tonnato

#2   serves 8

In heavy pan or Dutch oven heat
   2 *tablespoons olive oil*
Add and brown lightly on all sides
   1 *(3½-pound) boneless rolled leg of veal or rump*
Then add
   1 *large onion, thinly sliced*
   2 *(2-ounce) cans anchovy fillets*
   ½ *sour pickle*
   1 *(7-ounce) can tuna, drained*
   1 *cup dry white wine*
   2 *cloves garlic, cut in halves*
   2 *stalks celery, thinly sliced*
   1 *carrot, thinly sliced*
   3 *sprigs parsley*
   ½ *teaspoon thyme*
   1 *teaspoon salt*
   ¼ *teaspoon freshly ground pepper*

Cover and bring to boil. Reduce and simmer about 2 hours. Remove meat to large bowl and purée remaining ingredients. Pour
over meat and refrigerate overnight or longer. Remove meat and
make sauce by blending purée-marinade from which fat has been
removed with
   2 *tablespoons lemon juice*
   enough mayonnaise to give consistency of thin cream sauce

Just before serving carve the veal in very thin slices. Arrange on deep platter. Garnish with

    4 tablespoons capers

Pour sauce over veal.

Vegetables

Artichoke Bottoms Filled with Peas

serves 8

This is such a simple but delicious recipe, you'll wonder why you never thought of it before.

Drain contents of
    4 (11-ounce) cans artichoke bottoms (cans should have 8 to
        10 bottoms per can)
Heat the contents in
    butter
Meanwhile drain
    2 (1-pound) cans tiny peas
Heat them in
    butter
Spoon peas into artichoke bottoms and serve hot.

Artichoke Hearts and Peas

#1   serves 12

Thaw, then cut in half lengthwise, pat dry contents of
    2 (9-ounce) packages frozen artichoke hearts
Sauté hearts slowly until lightly browned in
    4 tablespoons butter

Add

> 2 (10-ounce) *packages frozen peas*
> 1 *cup water*
> 2 *tablespoons butter*
> 4 *teaspoons chopped parsley*
> ½ *teaspoon thyme*
> 2 *bay leaves*
> *few celery leaves*
> ¼ *teaspoon sugar*
> 2 *teaspoons salt*
> 1 *teaspoon pepper*

When ready to serve, cover pan and simmer over low heat for 25 minutes or until peas are tender and liquid has almost evaporated.

Baked Crusty Tomatoes

#1   serves 12

Combine

> ½ *cup butter*
> 2¼ *teaspoons seasoned salt*
> 1½ *teaspoons garlic powder*
> 1½ *tablespoons ground coriander*
> 1½ *tablespoons ground cumin*
> 1½ *cups cornflake crumbs*

Spread this mixture over cut side of

> 12 *small tomatoes, cut in half*

Place in shallow dish and refrigerate overnight. Bake at 300° for 30 minutes after letting tomatoes sit at room temperature for 10 minutes. Serve hot.

Betsy's Spinach

#1 serves 12

Melt in a 2-quart casserole
  1½ tablespoons butter
Combine and place in casserole
  3 packages frozen, chopped spinach, cooked and drained
  5 eggs, slightly beaten
  ¾ pound cottage cheese
  1½ tablespoons flour
  ¾ cup finely diced American cheese
  1½ teaspoons salt
  ¾ teaspoon pepper
  ½ teaspoon onion powder
  ½ teaspoon nutmeg
When ready to serve, bake at 325° for 45 minutes.

Broccoli San Vincente

#1 serves 8

Cook according to package directions
  2 packages frozen broccoli
Drain and place in a shallow baking dish.
Combine and spoon over broccoli
  ½ pint sour cream
  ½ cup shredded Cheddar cheese
  ½ teaspoon grated lemon rind
  1 tablespoon lemon juice
  ¼ teaspoon salt
  dash pepper
Sprinkle with
  ¼ cup toasted slivered almonds
When ready to serve, bake at 350° for 20 minutes until cheese begins to melt.

California Vegetable Bowl

#1   serves 12

In a large pot combine
> 8 cups sliced, unpared zucchini (about 4 pounds)
> 3 cups cut fresh or frozen whole kernel corn
> 2 medium onions, chopped
> ⅔ cup chopped green pepper

Add
> 2 teaspoons salt
> ¼ cup water

Cover and simmer, stirring occasionally, for 20 minutes or until vegetables are tender. Drain well. Add and toss lightly
> ¼ cup butter
> 2 tablespoons snipped fresh dill (or 2 teaspoons dried dill weed)

May be reheated at serving time.

Cauliflower with Caper Sauce

serves 6

Remove outer green leaves from
> 1 large head cauliflower

Break into flowerets. Place in saucepan with boiling salted water 1 inch deep. Bring to boil and simmer for 5 minutes or until cauliflower is tender. (If you wish you may cook 2 packages frozen cauliflower instead.) Drain liquid from cauliflower, reserving 1 cup. Blend together
> reserved liquid
> 1 tablespoon cornstarch

Add
>3 *tablespoons butter*
>3 *tablespoons lemon juice*
>1 *tablespoon grated onion*
>⅛ *teaspoon black pepper*
>1 *teaspoon turmeric*
>*salt to taste*

Cook, stirring, until sauce thickens. Add
>2 *tablespoons capers*

Pour sauce over cauliflower to serve.

Celery with Water Chestnuts

#1   serves 12

Slice into 1-inch pieces
>1½ *bunches celery*

Bring to a boil in saucepan with
>2½ *cups water*
>3 *chicken bouillon cubes*
>¾ *teaspoon basil*
>¾ *teaspoon salt*
>½ *teaspoon pepper*

Simmer about 10 minutes until still slightly crisp. Drain. Combine in a 2-quart casserole
>1½ (10-*ounce*) *cans cream of celery soup, undiluted*
>*cooked celery*
>2 (8-*ounce*) *cans water chestnuts, sliced*
>⅔ *cup sliced, blanched almonds*

Top with
>*buttered bread crumbs*

When ready to serve, bake uncovered at 350° for 30 minutes.

Lemon Pepper Tomatoes

serves 8

Slice horizontally in ½-inch-thick slices
    4 large tomatoes
Bread them lightly with
    ½ cup seasoned bread crumbs
Season them generously with
    freshly ground black pepper
    few drops lemon juice
    garlic salt
    minced onion
Dot each slice with
    butter
Broil until lightly browned.

Ratatouille

serves 8

Peel and thinly slice
    2 medium eggplants
Salt them lightly and pile together, weighting top of pile for ½
hour to remove excess juices. Then cut eggplant into small dice.
In a large skillet heat
    1 cup olive oil
Sauté in oil
    4 large onions, chopped fine
    4 green peppers, diced
    3 cloves garlic, minced
When vegetables begin to soften add
    8 ripe tomatoes, peeled and diced
    4 zucchinis, diced

Add
> salt and pepper to taste
> 3 tablespoons chopped parsley
> ⅛ teaspoon marjoram
> ⅛ teaspoon basil

Simmer for 30 minutes, until vegetables are soft but not mushy. Uncover and simmer 10 minutes more to reduce liquid. Serve hot or cold as a vegetable, or serve cold as an hors d'oeuvre.

Spanish Peas

#1   serves 12

Melt
> 6 tablespoons butter

Add
> 1½ teaspoons onion salt
> ¾ teaspoon orégano
> freshly ground black pepper

Cook for 3 minutes. Add
> 3 (1-pound) cans tiny green peas, drained
> 9 tablespoons chopped pimiento
> ¾ cup ripe olives, sliced

Toss lightly to mix. Refrigerate. To serve, cover and heat over low heat until peas are hot.

String Bean Casserole

#1   serves 6

Sauté until golden
> 2 tablespoons chopped onion
> 2 tablespoons chopped green pepper

in
>   2 tablespoons butter

Add
>   2 (1-pound) cans string beans
>   1 (1-pound, 12-ounce) can whole tomatoes
>   1 teaspoon salt
>   ⅛ teaspoon pepper

Place in a buttered 2-quart baking dish. Top with
>   8 saltine crackers, crumbled
>   ¼ cup grated American cheese

When ready to serve, bake covered at 350° for 25 minutes.

Zesty Butter Beans

2   serves 6

At a tasting party one of the guest-tasters suggested that green beans would do just as nicely in the sauce. Try it.

Combine
>   ¾ cup light brown sugar
>   ½ cup catsup
>   ⅓ cup dark corn syrup
>   2 to 3 teaspoons liquid smoke
>   1 medium onion, diced

Add
>   3 (1-pound, 4-ounce) cans large lima beans, drained.

Turn into 1½-quart casserole. Arrange
>   4 strips raw bacon on top

Refrigerate. To serve, return to room temperature, then bake at 325° for 1 hour.

Zucchini au Gratin

In bottom of 2-quart casserole, pour
    4 tablespoons olive oil
Cut into thin rounds
    6 medium zucchini
Cut into small cubes
    1 pound mozzarella cheese
Make layers in casserole, alternating zucchini, mozzarella and
    ½ cup grated Parmesan cheese
    salt
    chopped parsley
Top with
    1 cup bread crumbs
Dot with
    4 tablespoons butter
When ready to serve, bake uncovered at 350° for 1 hour until
golden brown.

Zucchini Casserole

Slice into ½-inch pieces
    9 young, small zucchini
Melt in a skillet
    1½ tablespoons butter
    1½ tablespoons oil

Add

> 1½ *cloves garlic, minced*
> 3 *tablespoons finely chopped onion*
> 1½ *tablespoons chopped chives*
> 1½ *tablespoons finely chopped celery*
> 1½ *tablespoons chopped parsley*
> 1½ *teaspoons dried dill*
> 1½ *teaspoons salt*
> ¾ *teaspoon pepper*
> ½ *teaspoon paprika*

Cook slowly until onions are soft. Combine and add to onion mixture

> 1½ *cups tomato-vegetable juice*
> 3 *tablespoons catsup*
> ¾ *teaspoon Worcestershire sauce*

In a large casserole, spread a little of the onion mixture and cover with slices of zucchini. Salt lightly, spoon over a little more onion and sprinkle with

> *Parmesan cheese*

Repeat layers, ending with sauce and cheese. When ready to serve, bake at 375° for 1 hour.

Potato, Noodle,
and Rice Dishes

Beer Barrel Potatoes

#2   serves 8

In a 1-quart casserole layer
  6 large potatoes, peeled and thinly sliced
  1½ cups chopped onion
  3 cups thinly sliced celery
Combine
  1½ cups beer
  1½ cups chicken stock
  1½ teaspoons salt
  ¼ teaspoon white pepper
Pour over potato mixture. Cover and bake at 375° for 1 hour. Remove from oven and let cool slightly. Refrigerate. To serve, return to room temperature and bake for 30 minutes more or until tender. Meanwhile combine
  ⅓ cup butter or margarine
  ¾ cup dry bread crumbs
  ⅓ cup grated Parmesan cheese
  ¼ teaspoon garlic powder
Uncover casserole; sprinkle with mixture and then with
  paprika
Continue to bake, uncovered, for an additional 10 minutes or until top is golden brown and potatoes are tender.

Elegantly Scalloped Potatoes

serves 8

Boil in their skins
> 6 *medium potatoes*

Cool, peel, and cut into julienne strips. In saucepan over low heat combine
> *2 cups shredded Cheddar cheese*
> *¼ cup butter*

Stir occasionally until almost melted.
Remove from heat and blend in
> *1½ cups sour cream*
> *⅓ cup chopped green onions*
> *1 teaspoon salt*
> *¼ teaspoon pepper*

Fold in potatoes and turn into greased 2-quart casserole. Refrigerate. To serve, return to room temperature and bake 25 minutes at 450° or until heated through.

Fruited Yams

#1   serves 12

Combine gently in a 3-quart casserole
> *3 (#2) cans yams, halved lengthwise*
> *1 (#2) can pineapple chunks, drained*
> *1 (#2) can sliced peaches, drained*
> *1 (#2) can apricot halves, drained*
> *1 (#2) can sliced pears, drained*
> *2 bananas, sliced*

Mix together and pour over all
> *1 cup mixed fruit juices*
> *1 cup brown sugar*
> *1 teaspoon nutmeg*

Dot with
> 3 tablespoons butter

Bake at 350° for 20 minutes.

Lisa's Noodles

* # 2   serves 10

In boiling salted water cook for 10 minutes
> 1 (8-ounce) package fine egg noodles

Drain. Combine
> 1⅔ cups small curd cottage cheese
> 1⅔ cups sour cream
> 1 clove garlic, minced
> ⅔ medium onion, finely chopped
> 5 teaspoons Worcestershire sauce
> 5 teaspoons sesame seeds
> salt to taste
> dash hot pepper sauce

Add to noodles and mix gently. Place in buttered casserole. Refrigerate or freeze. To serve, return to room temperature, then bake at 350° for 45 minutes. Serve with
> freshly grated Parmesan cheese.

Nutty Rice with Mushrooms

1   serves 12

Melt
> ½ cup butter

Add
> 1½ teaspoons curry powder

Sauté in this
> ¾ *pound mushrooms, sliced*
> 3 *tablespoons chopped green pepper*
> 3 *tablespoons chopped onion*

Add
> ¾ *cup coarsely chopped pecans*

Cook 1 minute, then add
> 4½ *cups chicken broth*

Then add
> 2¼ *cups long grain rice*

Place in 2-quart casserole. Bake at 325° for 1 hour until liquid is absorbed.

Pine Nut Bulgur

*#3   serves 12

Bulgur is cracked wheat that is usually prepared like rice, but it has a nutty flavor that makes it a delightful change from rice.
Melt
> 4 *tablespoons butter*

Sauté until transparent
> ½ *cup chopped onion*
> 4 *cloves garlic, minced*

Add and stir well
> 4 *cups cracked wheat* (*bulgur*)

Then add
> 4 *tablespoons chopped parsley*
> 1 *teaspoon powdered orégano*

Sauté 5 minutes, stirring once or twice. Add
> 8 *cups chicken bouillon or stock*

Cover casserole and refrigerate or freeze after liquid has been absorbed. To serve, bring to room temperature, then bake at 350° for 40 to 45 minutes, until well heated. Just before serving sprinkle over the top
> 1 *cup salted pine nuts.*

Salads and Cold Vegetables

Avocado and Hearts of Palm Salad

serves 12

Chill
   2 (14-ounce) cans hearts of palm
Wash, drain and pat dry
   2 heads Romaine lettuce
Peel and slice
   2 large ripe avocados
Drain hearts of palm and slice. Tear lettuce into bite-sized pieces and toss these three ingredients with Herb Dressing.

Herb Dressing:
Combine in blender
   1 cup olive oil
   6 tablespoons wine vinegar
   ¼ teaspoon powdered thyme
   ¼ teaspoon powdered marjoram
   ½ teaspoon dried basil
   2 tablespoons chopped onion
   2 tablespoons water
   1 teaspoon salt
   2 tablespoons chopped parsley

Best Beet Salad

2   serves 8

Combine and marinate at least 3 hours
  4 cups diced cooked beets
  2 cups chopped uncooked cabbage
  8 tablespoons white prepared horseradish
  4 teaspoons sugar
  2 teaspoons salt
  ½ teaspoon pepper
  1 cup vinegar
When well marinated, drain off liquid. Combine in top of double boiler
  4 teaspoons sugar
  1 teaspoon salt
  ½ teaspoon pepper
  6 tablespoons vinegar
  4 teaspoons butter
When mixture is warm, add
  4 eggs, beaten
Cook until thick, stirring. Cool and add
  6 tablespoons light cream
Combine with beets and cabbage and serve chilled.

Celery Heart Salad

1   serves 8

Wash and trim
  4 small celery hearts
Put celery in covered pan with
  2 small onions, sliced
  5 cups bouillon or chicken stock

Simmer 15 minutes. Let cool in stock. Remove hearts and cut in half lengthwise. Place in shallow dish. Add
  2 cups garlic-flavored French dressing
Chill. Drain off most dressing. Serve on
  shredded lettuce
Sprinkle with
  black pepper
Garnish with
  anchovies
  pimientos, sliced
  tomatoes, quartered
  ripe olives.

Chutney Cherry Ring

#2   serves 8

An unusual and delicious combination of ingredients.
Drain, reserving all liquid
  2 (1-pound, 1-ounce) cans pitted dark sweet cherries
Soften in the reserved liquid
  2 envelopes unflavored gelatin
Stir into the gelatin mixture
  3 tablespoons chopped chutney
  1 teaspoon grated orange rind
  1 (3-inch) cinnamon stick
  1 cup dry red wine
  2 tablespoons lemon juice
  1 tablespoon sugar
Heat mixture to boiling, stirring. Remove from heat, remove cinnamon stick and cool to lukewarm. Remove 1 cup of liquid and set aside. To remaining liquid add drained cherries. Turn into 1½-quart ring mold. Chill until firm. Meanwhile blend into reserved liquid
  1 pint sour cream
  ⅛ teaspoon salt

Spoon this mixture on top of thickened cherry mixture. Chill until firm. Unmold to serve.

Confetti Rice Salad

#3   serves 12

Combine and let stand while preparing remaining ingredients
>   7 *cups hot cooked rice*
>   ¾ *cup French dressing*
>   2¼ *teaspoons salt*
>   ¾ *teaspoon pepper*
Then add
>   1 *cup minced celery*
>   1 *cup minced green pepper*
>   ½ *cup minced sour pickles*
>   4½ *tablespoons capers*
>   4½ *tablespoons minced pimiento*
>   1½ *cups mayonnaise*
Toss lightly with fork and place in ring mold or any other desired mold. Chill thoroughly. To serve, unmold.

Cucumber Mousse

#1   serves 8

Cut in half lengthwise and remove seeds from
>   2 *cucumbers, peeled*
Blanch cucumbers for 5 minutes in
>   1 *cup boiling water*
>   1 *tablespoon lemon juice*
Drain well and put through blender. Cool and add

    1 *teaspoon* Worcestershire *sauce*
    ¾ *teaspoon salt*
    ½ *teaspoon pepper*
    ½ *cup mayonnaise*
Soften
    1 *envelope unflavored gelatin*
in
    1 *tablespoon cold water*
Dissolve in
    1 *tablespoon hot water*
and add to cucumber mixture with
    ½ *cup heavy cream, whipped stiff*
Add a
    few drops green food coloring
Turn into chilled ½-quart mold, chilling until firm.
Score with tines of fork and slice thinly
    1 *cucumber*
Marinate slices in
    French Dressing
Unmold mousse and arrange slices on top of mousse

French Dressing:
Combine and shake well
    ½ *cup wine or malt vinegar*
    ¾ *teaspoon salt*
    ¼ *teaspoon freshly ground pepper*
    1½ *cups olive oil.*

Dilled Potato Salad

#2   serves 6

Combine
    4 *cups diced cooked potatoes*
    1 *cup sliced celery*
    3 *green onions, sliced thin*

Mix together and pour over the potatoes
>   3 *tablespoons vinegar*
>   3 *tablespoons salad oil*
>   ¼ *teaspoon seasoned salt*
>   ¼ *teaspoon seasoned pepper*
>   ½ *teaspoon dry dill weed*

Refrigerate for several hours. Then mix in
>   ¾ *cup sour cream*
>   1 *green pepper, slivered.*

Ensalada de Arroz

#2   serves 8 to 10

Combine
>   ¾ *cup olive oil*
>   ½ *cup orange juice*
>   ½ *cup wine vinegar*
>   ¾ *teaspoon salt*
>   1 *tablespoon grated onion*
>   1½ *tablespoons minced parsley*
>   3 *tablespoons chopped pimiento*

Let sit for ½ hour. Add
>   2 *packages frozen artichoke hearts, cooked and drained*
>   2 *oranges, cut in sections and seeded*
>   6 *cups cooked, cooled rice*

Toss to blend and refrigerate. To serve, toss again and arrange on platter with
>   2 *tomatoes, cut in wedges*
>   2 *tablespoons capers*

arranged on top.

Green Bean Salad

#1 serves 12 to 15

Cook in 1 inch of boiling salted water, covered, until tender (about 25 minutes)

  3 pounds green beans, cut on angle into 2-inch pieces

Drain and cool. Toss beans with

  1 large onion, minced
  ¾ cup salad oil
  ⅓ cup wine vinegar
  1½ teaspoons salt
  ¼ teaspoon pepper
  3 tablespoons chopped anchovy fillets

Refrigerate. Serve from a clear glass bowl.

Just Peachy Salad

#3 serves 8 to 10

In saucepan combine

  1½ cups water
  12 whole cloves
  1 stick cinnamon

Cover and bring to boil; simmer 15 minutes. Remove cloves and cinnamon; add enough boiling water to make 6 cups. Dissolve

  2 (3-ounce) packages lemon gelatin

in hot liquid. Add

  syrup drained from (1 pound 13 ounce) can of peaches (reserving 1 tablespoon)
  enough water to make 1½ cups liquid
  ⅛ cup vinegar

Chill until slightly thickened. Pour a small amount into bottom of 2½-cup ring mold. Using part of

  1 (3-ounce) package cream cheese

make 6 small balls (½ inch in diameter) from it and alternate them in bottom of mold with
   6 *maraschino cherries*
   6 *cling peach halves, drained*
Chill until firm. Meanwhile chill remaining gelatin until it mounds on spoon. Combine with
   remaining cream cheese
   reserved peach syrup
   2 teaspoons lemon juice
   ⅛ cup mayonnaise
   dash salt
Pour over fruit and gelatin in mold. Chill. To serve, unmold.

Pineapple Daiquiri Mold

#1   serves 8 to 10

Absolutely marvelous—especially if you like daiquiris!
Soften
   2 envelopes unflavored gelatin
in
   ½ cup lime juice
Drain syrup from
   1 (14-ounce) *can pineapple tidbits*
Combine syrup with enough water to make 2 cups. Stir in
   1½ teaspoons grated lime peel
   ½ cup sugar
   ¼ teaspoon salt
Heat, stirring, to dissolve sugar. Add softened gelatin; heat and stir until dissolved. Cool. Stir in
   1 cup orange juice
   ½ cup light rum
Chill until mixture begins to thicken.
Cut in half and scoop into balls using French ball cutter or teaspoon
   1 *avocado*

Fold avocado and drained pineapple tidbits into thickened gelatin. Turn into 1½-quart mold. Chill until firm. To serve, unmold.
Garnish with
   greens, pineapple slice, cherries, if desired.

Piquant Asparagus

#3   serves 8

*This is an unusual variation on a vinaigrette sauce and just de-
licious.*
Combine and mix well
   2 tablespoons tarragon vinegar
   4 tablespoons cider vinegar
   ¾ cup vegetable oil
   2 tablespoons sweet pickle relish
   ⅛ teaspoon sugar
   2 teaspoons chopped parsley
   2 teaspoons chopped chives
Use this mixture over
   4 pounds cooked, drained asparagus
Allow to marinate overnight.

Salad Continental

#1   serves 8

Chop medium fine
   1½ cups toasted English walnuts
Sprinkle about ¼ cup of them in bottom of 1-quart mold.

Soften
> 1 *envelope unflavored gelatin*

in
> ¼ *cup cold water*

Dissolve by placing over hot water. Combine
> ⅔ *cup mayonnaise*
> ½ *teaspoon salt*
> 1½ *teaspoons dry mustard*

and stir into dissolved gelatin. Add remaining walnuts and
> 2 *cups grated Cheddar cheese*
> ½ *cup shredded Parmesan cheese*
> ¼ *cup crumbled Roquefort cheese*

Into this mixture fold
> 1 *cup heavy cream, whipped*

Turn into mold and chill until firm. To serve, unmold on lettuce-lined serving plate. Surround with fruit, if desired.

Salade du Riz

#2   serves 8 to 10

So attractive-looking and easy to prepare. No need for a green vegetable or starch when serving this.

Combine and mix well
> 3 *cups cooked, chilled rice*
> 1 *cup diced, cooked green beans*
> ¾ *cup chopped black olives*
> ½ *cup diced pimiento*
> *salt and pepper to taste*

Add
> *enough Vinaigrette Dressing to coat thoroughly.*

Refrigerate overnight to blend flavors. Before serving, mix well again, but gently.

Vinaigrette Dressing
Combine and shake well
   ½ *cup wine vinegar*
   ¾ *teaspoon salt*
   ¼ *teaspoon pepper*
   1½ *cups olive oil*
   1 *teaspoon each finely chopped green olives, capers, chives, parsley, and gherkins*
   yolk of 1 hard-cooked egg, chopped.

Sparkling Salad Mold

#1   serves 12

Drain thoroughly
   1 (*1-pound, 13-ounce*) *can fruits for salad*
   2 (*11-ounce*) *cans mandarin oranges*
Dissolve
   2 (*3-ounce*) *packages lime gelatin*
   2 (*3-ounce*) *packages lemon gelatin*
in
   4 *cups boiling water*
Cool slightly, then stir in
   4 *cups lemon-lime carbonated beverage*
Pour over drained fruits. Mold in 3-quart mold. Chill until firm.
Unmold to serve on
   lettuce.

Spiked Bean Salad

2   serves 10

Mix and marinate at least 24 hours
>   1 (*1-pound*) *can cut green beans, drained*
>   1 (*1-pound*) *can cut wax beans, drained*
>   1 (*1-pound*) *can plain kidney beans, drained*
>   1 *medium onion, sliced thin*
>   1 *green pepper, sliced thin*
>   ⅔ *cup salad oil*
>   ⅓ *cup vinegar*
>   1 *teaspoon salt*
>   1 *teaspoon pepper*
>   2 *tablespoons dark rum*
>   2 *tablespoons Burgundy or other dry red wine*

Sweet Pepper Rice Salad

2   serves 8

Combine
>   4 *cups cooked, cooled rice*
>   3 *large green peppers, diced*
>   1 *large ripe tomato, peeled, seeded and cubed*
>   2 *ribs celery, diced*
>   1 *bunch green onions, thinly sliced*
>   2 *cans anchovy fillets, diced*
>   2 *tablespoons chopped parsley*

Mix together and pour over rice mixture
>   ¼ *cup olive oil*
>   2 *tablespoons lemon juice*
>   1½ *teaspoons salt*
>   ¼ *teaspoon pepper*
>   2 *cloves garlic, minced*

Toss to mix. Refrigerate overnight to blend flavors. Toss again
before serving.

Tangy Cucumber Ring

#2   serves 8

In small bowl sprinkle
> ¾ *teaspoon salt*
> ⅛ *teaspoon white pepper*

over
> 3 *cups grated, peeled cucumber*

In medium bowl combine
> 4 *cups sour cream*
> 3 *tablespoons cider vinegar*
> 3 *tablespoons lemon juice*
> 1½ *tablespoons sugar*
> 6 *tablespoons chopped pimiento*
> 1½ *tablespoons chopped chives or green onion*

Sprinkle
> 3 *envelopes unflavored gelatin*

over
> ¾ *cup cold water*

Let soften. Then place over hot water; stir to dissolve completely.
Stir gelatin and cucumber into sour cream mixture; turn into 6-
or 8-cup ring mold. Refrigerate until firm, at least 3 to 4 hours;
overnight is better. To serve, unmold and garnish with salad
greens.

Tomato Aspic in Cheese Crust

#1   serves 12

Dissolve
>   2 (3-ounce) packages lemon-flavored gelatin
in
>   2½ cups boiling water

Add and mix well
>   2 (8-ounce) cans seasoned tomato sauce
>   3 tablespoons vinegar
>   4 teaspoons lemon juice
>   1 tablespoon Worcestershire sauce
>   1 teaspoon salt
>   dash pepper
>   dash hot pepper sauce

Chill until partially set. Meanwhile combine
>   2 cups finely crushed rich round cheese crackers
>   ½ cup melted butter or margarine

Press firmly into two 10-inch pie plates, building up sides.
Bake at 375° for 6 to 7 minutes; cool.
After gelatin mixture is partially set, stir in
>   1 cup chopped stuffed green olives
>   ½ cup chopped black olives
>   ½ cup sliced green onions

Pour gelatin mixture into cooled crust. Chill until firm. To serve, decorate with
>   black olive slices
>   dabs of sour cream.

Tomato Ring

#1 serves 10

Heat to boiling
 1¼ cups tomato juice
 1 cup water
Combine with
 2 (3-ounce) packages lemon gelatin
Stir until dissolved. Cool until syrupy, then add
 ½ pint sour cream
 1 cup mayonnaise
 3 tablespoons vinegar
 1 tablespoon prepared white horseradish
 1 teaspoon onion salt
 4 drops hot pepper sauce
Beat until smooth. Pour into 5-cup ring mold. Chill until firm.
When ready to serve, unmold and fill center with
 sliced cucumbers and onions marinated in
 1 cup vinegar
 ¼ cup sugar.

Wilted Cucumber Slices

#2 serves 12

Boil together for 5 minutes
 ¼ cup water
 1 cup white or cider vinegar
 2 teaspoons salt
 1 teaspoon pepper
 ½ cup sugar
Cool. Slice very thin
 4 cucumbers, peeled
Lay slices in a bowl and cover with above mixture. Refrigerate
at least 2 to 3 hours. To serve, drain and garnish with
 fresh snipped dill or dried dill weed.

Breads

Barbecued French Loaf

*#1   serves 8

Brush each biscuit from
    2 cans refrigerated buttermilk biscuits
with some of
    6 tablespoons bottled barbecue sauce
Then stand on edge on ungreased cookie sheet. Press together and shape ends to form long loaf. Brush the whole loaf with barbecue sauce. Sprinkle with
    sesame seeds
Bake at 350° for 30 to 35 minutes or until golden brown.
To prepare in advance, bake at 350° for 15 minutes. Refrigerate or freeze. To serve, return to room temperature, then bake at 350° for 15 to 25 minutes, until golden brown.

Cheddar Corn Bread

*#1   serves 8

Sift together
    1 cup flour
    1 cup yellow corn meal
    1 tablespoon baking powder
    2 tablespoons sugar
    1½ teaspoons salt

Add
> 2 eggs, beaten
> 1 cup milk
> 2 cups shredded sharp Cheddar cheese

Stir until just blended. Pour into well-greased, heated 1½-quart ring mold. Bake at 425° for 20 minutes. Serve warm with butter. Can be reheated.

Garlic Cheese Bread

* # 1   1 loaf

Slice evenly, cutting not quite through
> 1 loaf brown-and-serve French bread

Combine
> ¼ pound butter
> 1 clove garlic, crushed
> 1 teaspoon seasoned salt

Spread butter mixture between slices. Insert between slices
> ½ pound Provolone cheese, thinly sliced

Wrap loaf in foil and refrigerate or freeze. When ready to serve, bring to room temperature, then bake wrapped in foil at 350° for 15 minutes. Unwrap top and bake 15 minutes more.

Herb Pinwheels

* #1   makes 24

Blend together and let stand for 1 hour
  ½ cup softened butter
  ⅛ cup chopped parsley
  ¼ teaspoon orégano
  ⅛ teaspoon tarragon
  ⅛ teaspoon thyme
  ¼ small onion, minced
  ½ clove garlic, crushed
  dash pepper
Meanwhile mix together
  2 cups sifted flour
  1 tablespoon baking powder
  1 teaspoon salt
Cut in with fork or pastry blender
  ⅓ cup vegetable shortening
Stir in
  ¾ cup milk
Knead dough on floured board. Roll in 10 x 12-inch rectangle.
Spread with herb butter. Roll up from 12-inch side as for jelly roll
and seal seams. Cut roll into 24 half-inch pinwheels. Place in ungreased muffin pans.
Beat together and brush over tops of pinwheels
  1 egg
  1 tablespoon water
Bake at 425° for 10 to 12 minutes until golden brown. Reheat to
serve warm.

Herb Ring-a-Round

* # 1   serves 12

Melt
    ½ *cup butter*
Stir in
    1 *tablespoon mixed salad herbs*
    ¼ *teaspoon nutmeg*
Separate dough into 36 rolls from
    3 *packages refrigerated butter flake or gem flake rolls*
One at a time, dip rolls into butter mixture to coat both sides. In a single layer in buttered 9-inch pie plate stand them on edge, working from outside toward center, making a swirl. Bake at 375° for 20 minutes or until golden. Serve hot.

To prepare in advance, bake at 375° for 10 minutes. Refrigerate or freeze. To serve, bring to room temperature, then bake at 375° for 10 to 12 minutes, or until golden.

Italian Crescents

1   makes 16

Unroll and separate into 16 triangles
    2 *packages refrigerated crescent rolls*
Mix together
    ½ *cup bottled barbecue sauce*
    ½ *teaspoon Italian seasoning*
Cut crosswise into 16 2-inch wide strips
    4 *long slices mozzarella cheese*
Brush each roll triangle with sauce mixture; top with cheese strip. Roll up, following label directions. Place on ungreased cookie sheet. Bake at 375° for 20 minutes or until golden. Serve hot.

To prepare in advance, bake at 375° for 10 minutes. Refrigerate. To serve, return to room temperature and bake at 375° for 10 to 12 minutes, until rolls are golden.

Orange Rolls

1 serves 6

Combine
   ¼ *cup brown sugar*
   1 *tablespoon frozen orange juice concentrate, undiluted*
   1 *tablespoon butter, melted*
   ⅛ *teaspoon cinnamon*
Spread 2 teaspoons of mixture in bottom of each of 6 muffin cups.
Open and separate
   1 (*8-ounce*) *package refrigerator flake-style rolls*
Place 2 rolls on edge of each cup. Bake at 375° for 12 to 14 minutes until golden brown. Allow to stand in pan 2 to 3 minutes,
then turn upside down on a plate and serve warm. If preparing in
advance, leave in pan after baking and refrigerate. When ready to
serve, reheat at 375° for 5 minutes, then proceed as above.

Poppy Sesame Petal Loaf

1 serves 8

Make 4 evenly spaced cuts in each biscuit from
   2 *packages refrigerated plain or buttermilk biscuits*
cutting to within ½ inch of center; spread cuts slightly to resemble
petals. Place, with petals touching, in two rows on each cookie
sheet. Dip the end of a wooden spoon handle into
   4 *tablespoons melted butter*
Press into center of each biscuit, dipping into melted butter for
each one. Sprinkle
   poppy seeds
into buttered centers. Sprinkle
   sesame seeds
over all of biscuit. Bake at 375° for 20 minutes, until golden. Serve
hot.

To prepare in advance, bake at 375° for 10 minutes. Refrigerate. To serve, return to room temperature, then bake at 375° for 10 to 12 minutes, or until golden.

Savory Butterflake Loaf

* # 1   serves 12

Combine and mix well
   ½ cup softened butter
   1 cup grated Parmesan cheese
   1 tablespoon instant minced onion
   1½ teaspoons caraway seeds
   2 teaspoons minced parsley
Open and separate into rolls
   4 cans refrigerated butter flake dinner rolls
Spread each roll with seasoned butter. Stand on edge in two 9 x 5 x 3-inch loaf pans, making two rows in each pan. Bake at 375° for 30 to 35 minutes until deep golden brown. Loosen edges and turn out immediately.
To make in advance, bake at 375° for 15 minutes. Refrigerate or freeze. To serve, bring to room temperature and bake for 15 to 25 minutes at 375° until deep golden brown.

Smoky Bread

* # 3   serves 8

Cut diagonally into 1-inch slices
   1 (1-pound) loaf French bread

Combine and spread on slices
> ½ *cup soft butter or margarine*
> 1 *cup (4-ounce) shredded sharp Cheddar cheese*
> 1 *tablespoon chopped parsley*
> ½ *teaspoon hickory smoked salt or liquid hickory smoke*
>   *seasoning*
> 2 *teaspoons Worcestershire sauce*

Reassemble loaf and wrap securely in heavy-duty aluminum foil. Freeze or refrigerate. To serve, return to room temperature and bake at 400° for 15 to 20 minutes, or until cheese is melted.

Cakes

Almond Tart

serves 8

Blend in a bowl until consistency of rolled oats
1½ cups flour
1 tablespoon sugar
½ cup plus 1 tablespoon butter
Add to dough
1 egg, beaten
Form dough into a ball and roll out to line bottom and sides of a 9-inch spring-form, tart pan or flan ring. Prick pastry all over with fork. Line pastry with aluminum foil. Fill with uncooked beans or rice and bake 5 minutes at 375°. Remove beans and foil and bake 8 to 10 minutes more.

Beat together until pale and thick
3 eggs
¾ cup sugar
Fold in
1 cup finely grated blanched almonds
1½ tablespoons grated lemon rind
⅓ cup lemon juice
¼ teaspoon almond extract
Pour mixture into tart shell. Return to oven and bake 25 minutes until filling is set and lightly browned. Remove tart from oven. Cool. Spread with
⅓ cup apricot preserves
Decorate with
toasted slivered almonds.

Filbert Torte

*# 2   serves 8

Beat together well
   8 egg yolks
   1 cup sugar
Add
   1 cup finely chopped filberts or pecans
   4½ (1-ounce) squares semi-sweet chocolate, grated
   1 teaspoon instant coffee powder
   2 heaping tablespoons apricot preserves
   ⅛ teaspoon baking powder
Stir well.
Beat until stiff, then fold into nut mixture
   8 egg whites
Grease two 8-inch cake pans. Sprinkle them with fine dry bread
crumbs. Fill them with batter. Bake at 350° for 25 minutes. Refrigerate or freeze. To serve, bring to room temperature, spread
between layers
   ½ cup strawberry jam
Sprinkle top layer with
   ¼ cup chocolate shot
Then serve with
   dollops of whipped cream.

Fyrste Kake
(Scandinavian Tart)

*# 1   serves 8

Cream together
   ¾ cup butter
   ¾ cup sugar
Add one at a time, beating well
   3 egg yolks

Stir in
   2½ cups flour
   1 tablespoon baking powder
Add
   1 teaspoon almond extract
Reserving half a cup of dough, spread rest of dough over bottom
of 9-inch greased cake pan.
Beat until frothy
   3 egg whites
Gradually add
   1 cup sugar
Beat until stiff. Fold in
   1 cup blanched almonds, ground
   ½ teaspoon almond extract
Spread this over lined cake pan. Add to reserved dough
   2 tablespoons flour
Roll out on floured board and cut into strips. Lay strips in a lattice
pattern on top of almond mixture. Bake at 350° for 45 to 50 minutes. Serve with
   fresh or frozen strawberries or raspberries.

Grandmother's Coffee Cake

* # 1   makes 2, serves 12

Sift together
   2½ cups flour
   ¼ teaspoon salt
Cut in
   1 cup butter
Add
   3 egg yolks, beaten
   ½ teaspoon vanilla
Dissolve
   1 package dry yeast

in
    ¼ *cup warm water*
Stir in
    3 *tablespoons sugar*
Add yeast mixture to batter and stir well. Cover and chill over-
night. Remove from refrigerator.
Beat until stiff
    3 *egg whites*
Add to whites gradually and beat until soft peaks form
    1 *cup sugar*
Divide dough into two pieces. Roll each into rectangle 6 x 12
inches, ¼-inch thick. Spread the rectangles with the egg white
meringue. Cover the meringue with
    ½ *cup chopped nuts* (*walnuts or pecans*)
    ½ *cup raisins*
Roll as for jelly roll. Place on greased baking sheet. Let rise in a
warm, draft-free place for 15 to 30 minutes. Bake at 350° for 25
minutes.

Miracle Meringue Torte

#3 (up to one week!)   serves 10

Cream together
    ½ *cup butter*
    ½ *cup sugar*
Add one at a time and beat after each addition
    4 *egg yolks*
Add
    ¼ *cup rich whole milk or light cream*
    ½ *teaspoon vanilla*
Sift together
    1 *cup sifted cake flour*
    1¼ *teaspoons baking powder*
    ⅛ *teaspoon salt*

Add flour mixture to creamed mixture and beat at least 2 minutes.
Grease and flour two 9-inch-round layer cake pans. Spread batter
evenly in pans. Beat until stiff

    4 egg whites
    pinch salt

Gradually add

    1 cup sugar
    1 teaspoon vanilla

Beat 1 minute after all sugar is in. Spread meringue lightly on top
of cake batter, being sure it touches all sides of the pan.
On one of the layers sprinkle

    ¼ cup broken walnuts

Bake at 350° for 35 minutes. Allow cakes to cool in their own pans.
Set on racks. Will keep in refrigerator covered with plastic wrap
and will actually improve with age. When ready to serve, remove
from pans, fill with

    ½ cup strawberries crushed into
    ½ cup whipped cream

Top with

    big berries.

Mocha Icebox Cake

#2   serves 12

Line bottom and sides of 12-inch spring form with

    split ladyfingers (use 5 packages in whole recipe)

Soften

    1½ envelopes unflavored gelatin

in

    ½ cup cold water

Heat together, stirring until smooth

    1½ (6-ounce) packages semi-sweet chocolate bits
    ¾ cup strong coffee

Remove from heat. Add gelatin and stir. Add to chocolate mixture
> 6 egg yolks, *thoroughly beaten*
> ½ cup sugar
> ½ teaspoon salt
> 1½ teaspoons vanilla

Mix well and chill until slightly thickened. Beat until foamy
> 6 egg whites

Gradually add and beat until stiff
> ½ cup sugar

Fold whites into chocolate mixture. Also fold in
> 1½ cups heavy cream, *whipped*

In the spring form, alternate layers of chocolate mixture and lady-fingers. Chill at least overnight. To serve, remove sides from pan and top cake with
> 1½ cups heavy cream, *whipped*.

Orange Spongecake

#1   serves 10

Beat for 7 minutes
> 4 egg yolks
> ¾ cup water

Add and beat for 7 minutes more
> 1 cup sugar

Combine and fold in
> 1½ cups sifted cake flour
> 2 teaspoons baking powder
> ½ teaspoon salt

Add
> 1 teaspoon lemon juice
> 1 teaspoon vanilla

Fold in
> 4 egg whites, *beaten stiff*

Bake in two ungreased 9-inch round cake pans at 350° for 25 minutes. Cool in pans. When cool remove from pan and over bottom layer pour

    ½ cup orange juice

Cover with

    ½ cup orange marmalade

Put on top layer. Pour over it

    ½ cup more orange juice

When ready to serve, cover with

    1 cup heavy cream, whipped

Garnish with

    well-drained mandarin orange sections

Chill until serving time.

Super Bundt Cake

* # 2
                                            serves 12

A joy to behold, a treat to eat.

Cream together

    ½ cup butter

    ½ cup margarine

    1½ cups sugar

Separate

    4 eggs

Add yolks to sugar and butter all at once. Add alternately flour and milk, using in all

    3 cups sifted cake flour

    1 cup milk

Stir in

    1 tablespoon baking powder

Add

    1 teaspoon vanilla

    1 teaspoon lemon extract

    1 teaspoon almond extract

Fold in

    4 egg whites, stiffly beaten

Mix together for filling

    ½ cup sugar
    2 tablespoons unsweetened cocoa
    2 tablespoons cinnamon
    1 cup ground pecans
    ½ teaspoon almond extract
    grated rind 1 lemon
    grated rind 1 orange

Put ⅓ batter in well-greased 10-inch bundt pan. Add ½ filling. Melt

    ½ cup butter

Pour half butter over filling. Repeat process. End with batter. Bake at 350° for 65 minutes. Cool in pan.

Sweet Potato Pecan Cake

* # 1   serves 8 to 10

Divinely rich—very southern.

Combine

    1½ cups shortening
    2 cups sugar

Beat until smooth. Add and beat well

    4 egg yolks

Sift together

    2½ cups cake flour
    1 tablespoon baking powder
    ¼ teaspoon salt
    1 teaspoon cinnamon
    1 teaspoon nutmeg

Add the dry ingredients to first mixture along with

    4 tablespoons hot water

Stir in and beat well

    1 cup chopped pecans

    1½ cups grated raw sweet potatoes

    1 teaspoon vanilla

Beat until stiff

    4 egg whites

Fold into cake mixture. Bake in three greased 8-inch cake pans at 350° for 30 minutes. Cake may be frozen unfrosted.

#1

Frosting:

In saucepan combine

    1 (13-ounce) can evaporated milk

    ¼ pound margarine or butter

    1 cup sugar

    3 egg yolks

    1 teaspoon vanilla

Cook over medium heat about 12 minutes, stirring, until mixture thickens. Remove from heat and add

    1⅓ cups flaked coconut, unsweetened if possible

Beat until cool and of spreading consistency. Spread frosting between layers and on top and sides of cake.

Wellesley Coffee Cake

* #2   serves 12

Cream together

    1 cup butter

    2 cups sugar

Beat in one at a time

    2 eggs

Add and mix well

    1 cup sour cream

    ½ teaspoon vanilla

    ½ teaspoon almond extract

Combine and add
>   2 *cups sifted flour*
>   1 *teaspoon baking powder*
>   ¼ *teaspoon salt*

Combine for filling
>   4 *teaspoons sugar*
>   1 *cup chopped pecans*
>   1 *teaspoon cinnamon*

Place ⅓ batter in well-greased and floured 10-inch tube pan. Sprinkle with ¾ nut mixture. Spoon in rest of batter. Sprinkle with remaining nuts. Bake at 350° for 60 minutes.

Pies

Apricot Angel Pie

1   serves 8

Pie Shell:
Beat until frothy
    4 egg whites
Add
    ½ teaspoon salt
    ¼ teaspoon vinegar
Continue beating and add 1 tablespoon at a time
    1 cup sugar
Beat until stiff. Spoon into greased and floured 10-inch pie plate, shaping for pie shell. Bake at 275° for 45 minutes. Shut off heat and leave in oven for 30 minutes more. Cool.

Filling:
Sprinkle
    1 teaspoon unflavored gelatin
over
    2 tablespoons cold water
In top of double boiler combine
    4 egg yolks
    ½ teaspoon lemon rind
    5 tablespoons lemon juice
    ⅔ cup sugar
Beat well. Place over boiling water and cook until very thick (7 minutes) stirring constantly. Add gelatin and stir to dissolve. Add
    ½ pound dried apricots, cooked and puréed (about 1 cup)

Cool, then fold in
   1 cup heavy cream, whipped
Pour into shell. Refrigerate overnight. To serve, decorate with
   swirls of whipped cream
   toasted slivered almonds.

Coffee Almond Cream Pie

#2   serves 8

Crust:
Beat until stiff
   1 egg white
Add
   ¼ cup sugar
   ⅛ teaspoon salt
   1½ cups blanched almonds, ground fine
Line bottom and sides of 9-inch pie plate. Prick with fork. Bake
at 400° for 12 minutes, until brown.

Filling:
Combine in top of double boiler
   ½ cup water
   2 tablespoons instant coffee powder
   32 marshmallows
Stir constantly until mixture is smooth. Then add
   1 egg yolk, beaten
Stir for 1 minute. Cool by putting cold water in bottom of double
boiler and beat mixture until thick. When cool add
   1 teaspoon almond extract
Fold in
   1 pint heavy cream, whipped
Pour into crust. Sprinkle with
   ¼ cup slivered blanched almonds
Refrigerate at least overnight.

Orange Pecan Pie

* # 1 serves 8

Prepare
> *1 unbaked 10-inch pie shell*

Cut into quarters, seed and put through food grinder
> *1 whole orange, unpeeled*

Combine in saucepan
> *ground orange*
> *1½ cups packed light brown sugar*
> *1 cup light corn syrup*

Heat to boiling point, then remove from heat. Add and stir until melted
> *3 tablespoons butter*

Stir in
> *3 eggs, slightly beaten*
> *1¼ cups broken pecan halves*

Pour into unbaked shell. Bake at 350° for 45 to 50 minutes until set. Cool.

Cookies and Small Cakes

Almond Crisps

*#2   makes 36

Combine and mix well
- ⅔ *cup flour*
- ⅛ *teaspoon salt*
- ⅔ *cup sugar*
- ½ *cup soft butter*
- 1 *teaspoon grated lemon peel*
- 1 *cup blanched almonds, finely chopped*
- ½ *teaspoon vanilla*

Chill dough until firm enough to handle. Form dough into 1-inch balls and place 2 inches apart on ungreased baking sheet. Bake 8 to 10 minutes at 350°, until cookies are flat and have a brown, bubbly surface. Cool on pan for a few minutes before removing to cooling rack.

Almond Tea Cakes

*#3   makes 60

Mix together
- 1 *cup sugar*
- 2½ *cups flour*
- ½ *teaspoon salt*
- ½ *teaspoon baking soda*

Cut in with two forks or a pastry blender
   1 cup butter
Add
   1 egg, beaten
   1 teaspoon almond extract
Blend all with hands. Form into 1-inch balls and put on ungreased cookie sheets. On top of each cookie, press in
   half blanched almond
Bake at 350° for 15 to 20 minutes.

Cheese-filled Strudel

* # 2   serves 8

Bring to room temperature
   1 package phyllo leaves or strudel dough
Combine
   4 (3-ounce) packages cream cheese, softened
   ½ cup sugar
   3 egg yolks
Beat until well blended and smooth. Stir in
   ½ cup raisins
   2 teaspoons grated lemon peel
Refrigerate to firm up.
Keep phyllo leaves damp by placing on wax paper over damp towel and covering with damp towel.
Melt
   ⅓ cup butter
Brush one phyllo leaf with butter. Top with second leaf, brush with butter. Repeat this operation twice more, using four leaves all together. Spread ½ filling over ½ top leaf, starting from one short end. Then, from same end, roll up pastry jelly-roll fashion. Place roll on greased cookie sheet, seam side down. Brush with some of melted butter.
Repeat this operation, using remainder of leaves and filling. Bake

at 375° for about 30 minutes, until a golden brown. Cool on wire rack and freeze or refrigerate. To serve, return to room temperature and reheat in 200° oven for 10 minutes. Serve warm, cut in large slices.

Chocolate Mint Sticks

*#3   makes 36

Melt in top of double boiler
  2 (1-ounce) *squares bitter chocolate*
  ½ *cup butter*
Stir in
  1 *cup sugar*
  2 *eggs, beaten*
  ¼ *teaspoon peppermint extract*
Add
  ½ *cup flour*
  pinch salt
Mix thoroughly. Bake in greased 9-inch-square pan for 25 minutes at 325°. Cool.

Filling:
Stir until smooth
  2 *tablespoons butter*
  1 *cup confectioners' sugar*
  1 *tablespoon cream*
Spread filling over cooled cake. Refrigerate.

Glaze:
Melt in top of double boiler
  1½ (1-ounce) *squares bitter chocolate*
  1½ *tablespoons butter*
Drizzle glaze over cold firm filling, tilting pan back and forth until glaze covers all. Refrigerate or freeze. If frozen, partially defrost before slicing in squares. Keep in refrigerator until serving time.

Danish Sugar Cookies

*#3   makes 78

Whirl in blender a few at a time
 ½ cup blanched almonds
Cut
 ½ cup softened butter
into
 1 cup sugar
Stir in almonds and
 ½ teaspoon vanilla
 ½ teaspoon almond extract
Blend in with hands
 1 cup flour
Shape into two rolls. Sprinkle a little sugar on wax paper before using it to wrap dough. Chill. Slice ⅛ inch thick. Bake on ungreased sheets at 375° for 8 to 10 minutes.

Easy Schnecken

*#2   makes 24 tea-sized

Cream together
 4 tablespoons butter
 ¼ cup brown sugar
 1½ teaspoons white corn syrup
Coat miniature muffin tins heavily with this mixture. Place in each cup
 1 pecan half
Roll into 2 individual rectangles about 6 x 12 inches
 2 tubes refrigerator crescent rolls
Spread rectangles with mixture of
 ½ cup brown sugar
 1 teaspoon cinnamon
 ½ cup raisins
 ½ cup finely chopped pecans

Roll tightly as for jelly roll and seal seams. Slice each roll into 12 parts. Press into cups firmly. Let rise on top of oven until dough feels puffy (about 1 hour). Bake at 375° for 15 to 20 minutes until golden brown. Turn upside down immediately.

Frosted Walnut Bars

* # 2   makes 48

Work together with pastry blender
>   1 cup flour
>   ½ cup butter

Pat into 9 x 13-inch pan. Bake 12 minutes at 350°. Mix together
>   1½ cups brown sugar
>   2 tablespoons flour
>   ½ teaspoon vanilla
>   1 cup chopped walnuts
>   2 eggs
>   ¼ teaspoon baking powder
>   ½ teaspoon salt

Pour this mixture over baked crust. Bake 20 to 25 minutes more at 350°. Cool. Cream together
>   2 tablespoons butter
>   1½ cups confectioners' sugar
>   2 teaspoons lemon juice
>   2 tablespoons orange juice

Frost bars with above mixture. Cut into 48 bars.

Marble Brownies

*#2   makes 48

Melt over low heat, stirring constantly
  2 (4-ounce) packages sweet cooking chocolate
  6 tablespoons butter
Cool. Cream together until soft
  4 tablespoons butter
  6 ounces cream cheese
Gradually add
  ½ cup sugar
Stir in
  2 eggs
  2 tablespoons flour
  1 teaspoon vanilla
Beat until light and fluffy
  4 eggs
Gradually add
  1½ cups sugar
Fold in
  1 teaspoon baking powder
  ½ teaspoon salt
  1 cup flour
Blend in cooled chocolate mixture. Stir in
  1 cup chopped walnuts
  ½ teaspoon almond extract
  2 teaspoons vanilla

Measure 2 cups of chocolate batter and set aside. Spread rest of chocolate batter in greased 9 x 13-inch pan. Pour cheese mixture over top. Drop rest of chocolate by tablespoons onto cheese and swirl to marbleize. Bake at 350° for 35 to 40 minutes. Cool. Cut into bars.

Miniature Cheesecakes

* # 1 makes 42

Grease well with butter 42 tea-sized muffin tins. Dust the tins with
graham cracker crumbs
Combine thoroughly
2 (8-ounce) *packages cream cheese*
¾ *cup sugar*
3 *egg yolks*
grated rind 1 lemon
Beat until stiff, then fold in
3 *egg whites*
Spoon cheese mixture into tins and bake at 350° for 15 minutes.
Let cool on wire rack for 5 minutes. Centers will fall in slightly.
Combine the following and use 1 teaspoonful on top of each
cheesecake:
¾ *cup sour cream*
2 *tablespoons sugar*
1 *teaspoon vanilla*
Return cakes to oven for 5 more minutes. Cool completely before
removing from tins. Serve in paper baking cups.

Refrigerator Desserts

Apricot Mousse

#2   serves 12

Drain (reserving syrup) and purée in blender
    2 (1-pound, 14-ounce) cans apricots
Heat to boiling
    syrup from apricots plus water to make 3½ cups liquid
Add and dissolve
    2 (3-ounce) packages lemon gelatin
Add puréed apricots and
    2 tablespoons apricot brandy or Cointreau
Chill mixture until it begins to thicken, then beat it slightly. Fold in
    2 cups heavy cream, whipped
Pour mixture into a 10-inch spring form lined with
    2 packages ladyfingers, split
Refrigerate until set, at least 3 hours. Serve decorated with
    whipped cream
    apricot halves.

Baked Fruit Dessert

#2   serves 12

Spread in a 9 x 13-inch glass baking dish
>   2 (*1-pound, 13-ounce*) *cans pear halves, drained*

Top pears with
>   2 *pounds dried apricots*

Cover all with
>   2 (*8-ounce*) *cans raspberries with juice*
>   *juice and grated rind 2 lemons*
>   *juice and grated rind 2 oranges*

Sprinkle with
>   1½ *cups brown sugar*
>   ½ *cup Grand Marnier*

Bake at 350° for 1 hour. Chill and serve with
>   ½ *gallon vanilla ice cream, scooped into balls.*

Bernice's Most Heavenly Hash

#2   serves 8

Combine and refrigerate overnight
>   1 *pint heavy cream, whipped*
>   ½ *pound miniature marshmallows*
>   1 (*15½-ounce*) *can crushed pineapple, drained*
>   1 (*1-pound*) *can pitted black cherries, drained* (*reserve syrup*)
>   *about 3 ounces chopped walnuts*

Just before serving, stir in some cherry juice for color and flavor.
Spoon into dishes.

Frozen Macaroon Soufflé

*   serves 12

Soften
> 1 *quart vanilla ice cream*

Stir into ice cream
> 12 *almond macaroons, crumbled*
> 8 *teaspoons Grand Marnier*

Fold in
> 1 *cup heavy cream, whipped*

Spoon into 6-cup metal mold. Cover with plastic wrap and freeze. When ready to serve, unmold by running a knife around edge, then dipping mold quickly in hot water. Serve with Raspberry Sauce.

Raspberry Sauce:
Simmer until soft
> 2 (*10-ounce*) *packages frozen raspberries, defrosted*
> 5 *tablespoons sugar*

Stir in
> 8 *teaspoons Grand Marnier.*

Ginger Coffee Treat

2   serves 8

Cream until light and fluffy
> 1 *cup butter*

Beat in
> 2½ *cups confectioners' sugar*

Add, one at a time, beating well
> 8 *egg yolks*

Blend in
> ¼ *cup cold strong coffee*

Arrange a layer of
    gingersnaps
in bottom of small serving bowl or soufflé dish (about 1½-quart)
Combine
    2 tablespoons coffee
with
    1 tablespoon dark rum
Sprinkle a little on gingersnaps. Add layer of filling, then one of
gingersnaps, sprinkled with coffee-rum mixture. Continue until
filling is used, ending with gingersnaps.
Cover with aluminum foil and top with heavy weight like a brick.
Chill at least 24 hours before serving.

Paragon Queen's Heart

*   serves 8

Beat until light
    6 egg yolks
    ½ cup sugar
Stir in
    2 tablespoons Grand Marnier
Beat until stiff
    2 cups heavy cream
Fold the cream into the yolk mixture and pour into individual
heart-shaped molds. Freeze. To serve, unmold by dipping briefly
in cool water. Garnish with
    fresh strawberries or chocolate curls.

Royal Trifle

#1   serves 12 to 14

Sprinkle half of
>   6 *packages ladyfingers*

with
>   *rum*

Sprinkle the other half with
>   *crème de cacao*

Place a layer of rum-soaked ladyfingers in bottom of a 2-quart soufflé dish and a 1-quart soufflé dish. Spread with some of
>   1 (*12-ounce*) *jar raspberry preserves*

Add a layer of ladyfingers soaked in crème de cacao and spread with preserves. Repeat layering until dishes are filled.

Pour cooled Custard over ladyfingers and chill overnight. When ready to serve, top with
>   1 *cup heavy cream, whipped*

Custard:
Combine in heavy saucepan
>   8 *egg yolks, lightly beaten*
>   ½ *cup sugar*
>   4 *cups milk*

Beat with wire whisk to mix well. Heat over medium heat, stirring until mixture coats the back of a spoon. DO NOT ALLOW TO BOIL OR IT WILL CURDLE. Remove from heat and stir in
>   1 *teaspoon vanilla*

Cool to lukewarm.

Tia Maria Cold Soufflé

#2   serves 12

In saucepan stir until smooth
   ½ cup sugar
   1 cup water
   ½ cup plus 3 tablespoons Tia Maria liqueur
   2 tablespoons lemon juice
   1 envelope plus 2 teaspoons unflavored gelatin
   7 egg yolks
Cook over low heat, stirring, until it coats the spoon. Transfer to
large bowl and refrigerate until consistency of unbeaten egg
whites. Make a collar to fit around a 2-quart soufflé dish. Fold a
30-inch length of wax paper in half lengthwise and butter one
side of strip. Wrap, buttered side in, around soufflé dish so that
collar stands 3 inches above rim.
Drizzle
   2 to 3 tablespoons Tia Maria
over
   1 package ladyfingers
Line sides of soufflé dish with ladyfingers.
Into cooled gelatin mixture fold
   ¾ cup toasted slivered almonds
Whip
   2 cups heavy cream
Beat until soft peaks form
   7 egg whites
   ¼ teaspoon salt
Gradually add
   ¼ cup sugar
while beating stiff.
Fold both whites and cream into gelatin mixture and turn into
soufflé dish. Refrigerate. To serve, sprinkle with
   ¼ cup toasted slivered almonds.

Toffee Ice Cream Roll

Sift together
> ¾ *cup flour*
> 2 *tablespoons instant coffee powder*
> 1 *teaspoon baking powder*
> ¼ *teaspoon salt*

Beat until lemon colored
> 4 *egg yolks*
> 1 *teaspoon vanilla*

Add to yolks gradually and beat until thick
> ¼ *cup sugar*

Beat to soft peaks
> 4 *egg whites*

Add to egg whites gradually and beat until stiff
> ½ *cup sugar*

Fold yolk mixture into whites. Fold in dry ingredients. Spread in greased and wax-paper-lined 10 x 15-inch pan. Bake at 375° for 12 minutes. Turn cake out onto a dish towel sprinkled with
> *confectioners' sugar*

Peel off the wax paper and trim crusts. Roll cake up on its length in the towel. Cool on rack. Unroll cake, remove towel and spread with
> 1 *quart softened vanilla ice cream*

Sprinkle with
> 1 *cup chopped chocolate-covered toffee bars*

Roll up tightly and wrap in foil. Store in freezer until ½ hour before serving.

Index